From Blogs to Bombs

From Blogs to Bombs

The Future of Digital Technologies in Education

Mark Pegrum

UWA PUBLISHING

First published in 2009 by
UWA Publishing
Crawley, Western Australia, 6009
www.uwap.uwa.edu.au

 THE UNIVERSITY OF
WESTERN AUSTRALIA
Achieving International Excellence

A full CIP record for this book is available from the National Library of Australia
ISBN: 978-1-921401-34-3

Typeset in 10pt Bembo
Printed by Griffin Press

For Stephen

CONTENTS

Contents

ACKNOWLEDGEMENTS

A book like this has, naturally, been shaped by conversations over many years with colleagues, students and friends (including many who fit into two or even all three of the above groups) in venues ranging from classrooms to conference halls and channels ranging from webmail and Facebook to Twitter and Skype. I'd like to particularly thank those who took time out of busy schedules to comment on earlier drafts of this work: Margaret Adamson, Lisa Cluett, Jim Coleman, Mirjam Hauck, Sandy Heldsinger, Amy Hightower, Sarah Hopkins, Charles Lancaster, Rosemary Lancaster, Gary Motteram and Vance Stevens. I've also benefited from discussions of this project with Stephen Bax and Gavin Dudeney. All provided useful feedback which helped enrich my ideas and clarify my arguments. Any shortcomings, however, remain entirely mine. I'd also like to thank my patient proofreaders: Stephen Morris, Brian Pegrum and Margaret Pegrum. Finally, I'm indebted to Olivier Breton, my efficient and accommodating editor at UWA Publishing.

Unlike digital technology, which continues to evolve at breakneck speed, books eventually have to take a fixed form. The cut-off point for this book was around mid-July, 2009. For updates after that point, please feel free to take a look at the *E-language* wiki or follow my Twitter feed, as detailed at the end of the book.

KEY ABBREVIATIONS

artificial intelligence	AI
Advanced Research Projects Agency Network	ARPANET
computer-assisted language learning	CALL
Creative Commons	CC
electronic learning	e-learning
electronic portfolio	e-portfolio
electronic waste	e-waste
information and communication technologies	ICTs
instant messaging	IM
internet service provider	ISP
information technology	IT
One Laptop Per Child	OLPC
peer-to-peer	p2p
personal computer	PC
personal learning environment	PLE
professional–amateur	pro-am
really simple syndication	RSS
short message service	SMS
textspeak	txtspk
user-generated content	UGC
virtual learning environment	VLE
virtual private network	VPN

Many lenses

An introduction

There was a time when students began essays about their holidays with phrases like 'During the holidays...' or 'Over the term break...' Many still begin that way. So imagine the surprise of a teacher in the west of Scotland who, wading through students' essays in 2003, came across this text:

> My smmr hols wr CWOT. B4, we usd 2 go 2 NY 2C my bro, his GF & thr 3 :-@ kds FTF. ILNY, its gr8. Bt my Ps wr so {:-/ BC o 9/11 tht they dcdd 2 stay in SCO & spnd 2wks up N. Up N, WUCIWUG − 0. I ws vvv brd in MON. 0 bt baas & ^^^^. AAR8, my Ps wr :-) − they sd ICBW, & tht they wr ha-p 4 the pc&qt... IDTS!! I wntd 2 go hm ASAP, 2C my M8s again. 2day, I cam bk 2 skool. I feel v O:-) BC I hv dn all my hm wrk. Now its BAU ...[1]

It's on topic. It's a narrative of sorts. It's reasonably coherent. It conveys its message forcefully, if a little unsubtly. But can you read it? If you can't, you're far from alone. Many people who aren't 'digital natives'[2] − who don't belong to the 'net generation'[3] − struggle with it. The teacher, too, was stumped, comparing the text to hieroglyphics.

In more standard English, the opening might read: 'My summer holidays were a complete waste of time. Before, we used to go to New York to see my brother, his girlfriend and their three screaming kids face-to-face. I love New York; it's great'.[4] But clearly, whatever other conventions this text adheres to, it's not standard English. It's an example of what's commonly known as 'textspeak', or even 'txtspk'. Reported initially in Britain's *Sunday Herald*, the story caused a minor sensation in the UK press before spreading rapidly around the Anglophone world, being picked up by news outlets from CNN to *The Sydney Morning Herald*. In addition to making its way through traditional media channels on every continent, it also began to circulate virally on the web. Even today, a Google search for the first sentence of the essay produces hundreds of hits, with commentary available in German or Hebrew, Chinese or Vietnamese.

There's certainly a problem here – but what kind of problem is it? On one level, it's a technological issue. The keypads of mobile phones don't allow you to conveniently compose long sentences. Kids who text or SMS each other (to use two verbs now emerging from their infancy) are often in a hurry. What's more, the cost of sending a text may depend on its length. The use of shortened forms and pictographic representations – which do bear superficial similarities to Egyptian hieroglyphics, as the teacher observed – can save time and money. It's no wonder, then, that this kind of shorthand has developed to fit the medium, though it's also spread into emails and onto social networking sites where, since keypad and cost issues don't apply in the same way, it presumably fulfils a variety of other needs. Speed, as we'll see, is just one of these.

On a second level, the issue is pedagogical. The teacher was horrified, stating: 'I could not quite believe what I was seeing'. A representative of the Scottish Parent Teacher Council recommended to the *Sunday Herald* that: 'There must be rigorous efforts from all quarters of the education system to stamp out the use of texting as a form of written language so far as English study is concerned'.[5] A publisher cited by the BBC spoke about a 'degree of crisis' in the written English of university students.[6] Certainly there are linguistic and pedagogical concerns. However, the fundamental problem with this text is actually one of appropriacy for its *con*-text. In the midst of the ensuing 'uproar about falling literacy standards', Hamish Norbrook, writing in *The Guardian Weekly*, wondered whether texting might in fact present opportunities for English teachers to engage their students in writing tasks to help them recognise different linguistic registers.[7] Reminding us of Shakespeare's own 'famously inconsistent' spelling, the BBC reflected on whether txtspk could 'mean the liberation of our use of language'.[8] Writing in *The Sunday Times* some time later, Jeremy Clarkson noted that there are many historical precedents for changing the way we transcribe our language.[9] The expression of such contradictory opinions within the debate over txtspk shows the need for educators to explore the underlying issues in more detail. At the same time it's emblematic of the polarisation of conservative and liberal opinion around new forms of literacy, a polarisation which, if bridges are not built, threatens to halt all conversation on the subject.

But in the outcry over falling standards, pedagogical discussions began to shift to a third level: for this is also a social issue, as clearly demonstrated by the amount of media attention it received. In the popular imagination, language standards have long been linked to social and moral standards, of which they are seen as both symbol and guarantor. Since at least the days of Jonathan Swift, grammar has been treated as a buffer against social change, one that needs to be (re-)erected in the wake of any period of liberalisation. Whatever the limitations of the complaints tradition, there are important social issues to be addressed here. It's hard to imagine that naivety regarding context was the sole reason the student handed in such a text. Language, of course, is intimately bound up with identity. Was this a genuinely exploratory performance on the part of a relative newcomer in a linguistically unstable world? Or was it a linguistic rebellion of the kind teenagers have long engaged in – in this case, a digital native student intentionally throwing down the gauntlet to a 'digital immigrant' teacher? Or both?

To give Swift and his descendants their due: there's no doubt that language does codify power relations and, whatever the underlying cause, submitting an essay in txtspk suggests a flattening of the traditional hierarchies which formerly required careful, respectful interaction with authority figures like teachers. Later media discussions of txtspk show that the Scottish essay was just the tip of a looming iceberg. In early 2008, for example, the TV talkshow *Insight* cited examples from the Australian context, including a message received by a recruiter from a job candidate which read: 'thanx 4 ur call re intaview, c u then', while a less grateful new employee wrote simply: 'job sux – not coming back'.[10]

And so the social level, which pertains to individual and group relations within a given society, leads onto a fourth, sociopolitical level, where we have to ask deeper questions about social structures which we've long taken for granted. Some observers argue that far from being flattened, these structures are as entrenched as ever. From this point of view, txtspk essays or messages to recruiters reveal, more than anything else, the socioeconomic status of their writers, who may lack the educational or social sophistication to codeswitch appropriately. In other words, the so-called 'digital divide' is as much a literacy issue as an economic one. The new markers of class are not the presence or absence of technology, but facility and subtlety in its use.

And yet ubiquity of technology, too, is becoming a class marker. Ironically, an ability to switch off, to take technology-free holidays, is increasingly likely to signal high socioeconomic status and to be associated in the long term with healthier bodies and, especially, healthier minds. Stress-related illnesses are on the rise. Internet addiction clinics are starting to open around the world. As with any nutritional regime, an unbalanced digital diet will eventually have biological consequences. Such issues are part of a fifth, ecological level, which encompasses the health of the mind and the body as well as that of the biosphere to which we all belong. Maybe not every encounter with *baas* & ^^^^^ (sheep and mountains) should be mediated by technology!

The worldwide attention sparked by a schoolgirl in the west of Scotland in 2003 is thus symbolic of our time and the confusion we face over the direction of technological development and its implications for education. It's clear that we can examine the issues through a variety of lenses, each of which brings certain aspects into sharp focus while blurring others. Through a *technological lens*, we note the importance of mobile phone technology and its accompanying freedoms and restrictions. Through a *pedagogical lens*, we observe disagreements over literacy and how it should be taught. Through a *social lens*, we recognise processes of identity building, which may include bucking against established standards. Through a *sociopolitical lens*, we discover fundamental questions about social stratification and whether it's being undermined or, paradoxically, reinforced. Through an *ecological lens*, we're confronted with the limitations of our biology.

To develop a more sophisticated understanding of the intersections of technology and education, it's essential that we take the time to look through all of these lenses.

Five lenses

The term 'digital technologies' encompasses a range of information and communication technologies (ICTs), with particular emphasis on the internet and the computers or mobile devices used to access it. These technologies are among the most widely discussed subjects of our times: talked about in living rooms, conference rooms and boardrooms; in magazine features, talkback radio programs and TV chatshows; and, self-referentially, on homepages, blogs and wikis. They have a particular salience for education, in which, year on year, they're coming to play an ever larger role. It's hard to avoid the conclusion that technology and education have a tightly intertwined future. Unsurprisingly, this is a subject of interest to teachers and academics in all parts of the education system, but it's also of immediate relevance to students, of some concern to parents, and of considerable significance to politicians, journalists, social commentators and the general public who, understandably, feel they have a major stake in the future of education.

Predictably, lots of discussions of educational technology are focused through a *technological lens*, which emphasises the technology's capabilities, limitations and ongoing evolution – as web 1.0 is trumped by web 2.0, homepages migrate to blogs, email cedes to instant messaging, and terms like 'downloads' and 'mashups' become part of everyday language. Love it or hate it, technological development is proceeding apace. Treading water is not an option. The technological wave will carry us with it. But neither fear of the wave, nor awe at its size and power, will get us very far. Instead, we need to find ways to harness its energy so that, as we ride it, we can attempt to give our journey at least some direction of our own choosing.

First, though, we have to understand that 'technology' is about a lot more than technology. This realisation, to which many educators have come in recent years, was succinctly captured in a statement made at a 2007 technology conference in Chennai, just down the road from Bangalore, the burgeoning IT centre of India. It's essential, argued Gary Motteram and Sophie Ioannou-Georgiou in their plenary, that we remember the three Ps of e-learning: pedagogy, pedagogy and pedagogy![11] That the point needed to be made so forcefully shows it hasn't always been as obvious as it now seems; and what's more, that it may still not be obvious to everyone.

Looking at digital technologies through a *pedagogical lens*, rather than just a technological lens, allows the conversation to expand beyond the capabilities of the hardware and software. In discussions of the pedagogical approaches best suited to e-learning, it's often argued that the newer web 2.0 technology is an ideal vehicle for the social constructivist approaches that have shaped Western educational thought over the last few decades. Yet this sits uncomfortably with politically driven back-to-basics movements which, promising to leave no child behind, have recently swept much of the English-speaking world. Lines of conflict have opened up between education departments and governments, between teachers and parents, between universities and the media. Nor do educators speak with one voice: differing opinions reflect differences in fields of expertise, disciplinary allegiance and political persuasion.

In this context, we need to ask what changing pedagogy and tools will mean for recognised authority and established truth, as information and knowledge lose their traditional gatekeepers, literacy multiplies into multiliteracies, and languages spawn new registers. What are the consequences of collaborative, interactive educational approaches superseding individualist, transmission–oriented approaches? How should educators accommodate the emerging model of collective intelligence, of which we hear whisperings across the web? Is there any way to reconcile the views of the academics who eagerly, if sometimes uncritically, anticipate the benefits of 'the greatest unplanned collaboration in human history'[12] with the concerns of those who insist that 'Internet learning has, so far, been a tragedy for education'?[13]

But technological and pedagogical lenses, even used in complementary fashion, won't satisfy the inquiring gaze of the media. It's all very well for technologists to talk about advances in speed and flexibility. It's all very well for teachers, disagreements notwithstanding, to extol the constructivist virtues of online tools. The media, however, channel the social anxieties of the wider community. It's true that some media conduits like *Wired* frequently carry celebratory reports of the new technologies. Others, such as *The Guardian* or *The Economist*, take a more neutral or nuanced approach. But it's hard not to notice that our newsstands, airwaves and, ironically, more than a few websites are brimming over with an angst that sometimes verges on panic, mostly centred on a perceived need to protect the younger generation.

Of course, it's crucial that the media apply a *social lens* to the phenomenon of digital technologies, introducing into national and international conversation the most pressing issues, negative as well as positive. This has to include some consideration of the dangers for young people of lives increasingly lived online: predation, cyberbullying and compromised privacy, to name a few. All are important matters. All, unfortunately, are also red rags to the injured bull of public hysteria. It's worth remembering, for example, that there have been more articles published about MySpace predators than there have been predators reported.[14] The greatest danger, however, is not that hysteria is uninformed or even unproductive, but that it smothers more thoughtful approaches, making balanced discussion extremely difficult.

Yet thoughtful, balanced discussion is very much needed, not only on the negatives for young people, but on other possible negatives

– and the possible positives – and the unknowns. Fortunately, thanks to more reflective commentators, other important social questions are being articulated. What are our online options for maintaining old social ties, making new ones, or avoiding either or both? How should we behave when, amid tricky context collisions,[15] we find ourselves simultaneously networked with our current partner, our ex-partners, our family, our friends, our colleagues…and perhaps a future employer to boot? What does it mean to be submerged in a 24/7 data stream and to multitask endlessly, operating in a state of continuous partial attention?[16]

And what exactly *is* this net generation emerging before our eyes? It will be, in some ways at least, quite unlike preceding generations. It will have new ways of establishing and affirming identity, which may strike older generations as anything from self-assured to self-indulgent. It will have new ways of expressing its views as it peppers the digital landscape with user-generated content and remixes. It will have new ways of socialising and bonding, perhaps uniting a transient teenage passion for kicking against authority with a long-term preference for hooking into non-hierarchical networks. It will have new attitudes to security and privacy, which may yet turn out to involve empowerment and delusion in equal measure. And at the root of it all, it will have very different attitudes to technology. As one student told Marc Prensky: 'You look at technology as a tool. We look at technology as a foundation – it's totally integrated into what we do'.[17]

On the other hand, we'd be unwise to expect that any new generation will differ completely from its predecessors. In the face of complex and mounting challenges, where the negatives and positives are frequently intertwined, we can stand on the sidelines and watch or, worse still, we can drive the net generation's use of digital technologies underground by banning their use in schools and public libraries. The alternative is to listen to and learn from what the net generation has to say, and at the same time do our best to offer some careful guidance and some measured warnings. In other words, we – educators, parents, carers, counsellors, researchers, politicians or journalists – can invest something of ourselves in a partnership with the young people who will in time become fully fledged citizens of our own societies. When, as adults, they look back, they may not have much comprehension of how or why we were willing to let the rampaging bull of public hysteria shape social and educational agendas for so long.

Discussions of the social aspects of digital technologies inevitably begin, at their fringes, to touch on political and structural issues. If we refocus through a *sociopolitical lens*, we see that some of the shadowy concerns which have hovered insistently at the edges of our vision as we've peered through technological, pedagogical and social lenses are suddenly thrown into sharp relief. We find ourselves facing far-reaching and at times quite disturbing questions about how our societies are structured; how our societies relate to other societies; and just how stable our internal social structures and external social relations are.

In some Western countries, the internet has been gaining traction as an interactive channel for political candidates, local and state governments, and even federal governments. The net played a significant role in galvanising the youth vote in the Australian general election of 2007 and the US general election of 2008. In 2008, the Australia 2020 summit was perceived by some as the beginning of a move towards 'technologically enabled talk back government' in Australia.[18] In the UK, the Shadow Chancellor has spoken of using the web to open-source policy, in an effort to draw ideas from the public.[19]

At the same time, the net and mobile technologies have opened up new options for those whose voices aren't heard in regular political forums, or for whom no regular political forums exist. 'Smart mobs', to use Howard Rheingold's term, organise themselves organically, without any hierarchical or centralised control, to create large-scale protests which sometimes precipitate dramatic political changes.[20] Manila, 2001. Madrid, 2004. More recently, during the Beijing Olympic Torch Relay of 2008, the internet ran white-hot. Opposing interest groups sprang up on Facebook. Pro-Tibetan protests flowed from the streets of Paris and San Francisco onto the virtual islands of Second Life and back again. Pro-Chinese demonstrations spilled out of cyberspace chatrooms and onto the streets of Canberra and Seoul.

OK, it may all be a little rough and ready, but so far it sounds like a blueprint for a robust, technologically enabled network society where everyone's voice is heard. However, there's a flip side. Vigilante groups can spring up online, as in the wake of the Australian bushfires in early 2009. Chinese 'human flesh search engines' are known to scour the country for perceived transgressors of social norms. Islamic fundamentalists issue death threats to Western video hosting services like LiveLeak. And then there are the bombs that shake the world. London, 2005. Mumbai, 2008. Nowadays nation states, the traditional building blocks of the world order, share the stage with vigilantes and terrorists, all of whom, thanks to technology, can act without state sanction.

But we also need to ask some uncomfortable questions about state policies and practices. Amid the cacophonous babble of cyberspace, who is silent? Who falls on the wrong side of the digital divide, within the West and beyond it, as neocolonial relations play themselves out online and offline? Who doesn't get to shop in the multicultural marketplace beckoning at the end of history? And which views can't or won't be expressed as governments across the political spectrum isolate and gag the voices they fear – while tracking the rest, just in case?

The twentieth century also left us with a legacy of global issues which exist beyond political and ideological polarities. And so we come, finally, to the need to observe technology through an *ecological lens*. What are attention-hungry technologies doing to our minds and bodies? What are energy-hungry devices and their e-waste doing to the larger ecosystem of which we're part? It's a race against time. In the face of clashing cultures, divisive markets and suspicious governments, is the collective global awareness facilitated by the internet developing quickly enough to offset the mounting problems of neglected bodies, overloaded minds and, above all, a poisoned world?

From blogs to bombs

It's long been understood that the area of digital technologies in education covers education *through* digital technologies. However, it must also, crucially, encompass education *about* digital technologies and their effects, positive and negative, known and unknown, predictable and unpredictable. The results of a lack of understanding of our technologies are already becoming all too apparent.

Digital technologies, as we've seen, lend themselves to viewing through at least five lenses: the technological, the pedagogical, the social, the sociopolitical and the ecological. As with any set of lenses, there's considerable overlap in what the various lenses enable us to see, but there are also differences in what comes into clearest focus and what's relegated to a blurrier presence. So, even allowing for overlap, a minimum of five lenses seems necessary to capture the focal points of the main conversations we've been having, and need to have, about new technologies in education: the technological discussions typically favoured by IT professionals and some educators; the pedagogical discussions favoured by many academics and teachers; the social discussions favoured by the media and politicians; the sociopolitical discussions favoured by cultural and political theorists; and the ecological discussions which are beginning to take place among scientists and medical researchers, and are just starting to reach public consciousness.

The broad issues that come into focus through each of the lenses are informed by a range of more specific topics that crystallise at different resolutions. The model in Figure 1.1 attempts to capture some of the key issues and topics, arranged across five levels. Like all models, it involves a trade-off between detail and depth on the one hand, and clarity of presentation on the other. Inevitably, it entails some simplification, but its main aim is not to simplify our conversations. On the contrary, the aim is to lead us away from simplification by reminding us of the many issues which have an impact on, or are impacted by, the use of digital technologies in education. The terms employed are largely drawn from common usage, with some referring to developments and others to trends or problems, some to theories and others to fields of study or debate. Some are widely accepted and others are controversial. Some are relatively neutral and others carry positive or negative overtones. Closely related issues often cluster together, with issues at one level feeding into and articulating with issues at other levels. While some phenomena are shown on lens boundaries, most can be viewed through multiple lenses, with each lens highlighting particular aspects.

The model also functions as an overview of the key issues addressed in this book although, because of close connections between issues in different areas, they won't always, or only, be discussed within the most obviously relevant chapters. Nor is the list of topics exhaustive, though it includes many of the most important ones for educators. Those which will feature more prominently in our discussion are shown, in the style of a tag cloud, in larger and darker (bold) fonts. As with most tag clouds, this represents a personal perspective, a snapshot of new technologies in education taken from one point of view among the constellation of possible points of view, though it does draw extensively on the views of others working in the field. Of course, the model is a work in progress and, like digital technologies themselves, will be subject to constant revision – notwithstanding the requirements of print, which freezes it at a certain moment in time.

The model, then, is a reminder that the issues which have an impact on digital technologies in education – that is, education *through* and simultaneously *about* digital technologies – run from blogs to bombs, from technology to politics, and back again, while encompassing a host of other areas at the same time. It's a reminder that we need to develop a more holistic view of digital technologies in general, and as they apply to education in particular. That's the only way we can hope to grasp what new technologies may mean for the individual and communal stories which we can, and cannot, tell about ourselves.

Telling stories

In the past, an individual's life narrative was largely determined by his or her role within traditional institutions like the family and the church. But in modern liberal democracies, where external sources of identity are fewer and weaker, individuals are increasingly compelled – that is, empowered but also obliged – to author their own life stories.[21] It's a process which has been underway for some time but was given a major boost in the social revolutions of the late 60s. Even if institutional power has become more subtle rather than disappearing, and even if consumerist pressure has expanded to fill some of the gaps, there's no doubt that all around us we see individuals choosing ways of life unthinkable in past eras. Naturally, we also tell collective stories: stories of the groups, communities, and nations to which we belong. Here, too, we see a profound change, although once again it's relative rather than absolute. A multitude of individuals now find themselves in a position to actively contribute to the communal stories with which their personal stories are interwoven, and simultaneously to reject those communal stories to which they can't or don't want to contribute.

Enter digital technologies, which further diminish limitations on individual agency by offering us a panoply of tools for constructing our personal stories as well as multiplying the channels we can use to connect with chosen others and compose communal stories. Indeed, it

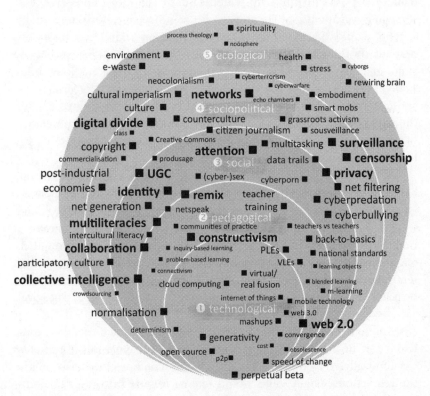

Figure 1.1. Five lenses on digital technologies in education.

11

should come as no surprise that contemporary digital technologies are the fruit of seeds planted in the rich soil of the revolutionary period at the end of the 60s. Today, individuals find themselves empowered to express themselves verbally on Blogger, visually on Flickr, and in video remixes on YouTube; to experiment with identity under cover of anonymity in ICQ ('I seek you') chatrooms or in Second Life; and to carve out social networks unrestricted by geography or tradition on Facebook or MySpace. Groups find themselves empowered to build collaborative wikis or Creative Commons repositories; to leverage networks for grassroots social initiatives; and to organise themselves into political smart mobs.

But the plot of this technological tale has lots of twists and turns, many of which, as we've seen, have little to do with technology itself, and we're still a long way from any kind of conclusion. We have to recognise that digital technologies don't just offer narrative freedom to artists mashing up media content, teens coming to terms with their sexuality, or anti-poverty campaigners; they offer the same freedom to vigilantes, child pornographers and terrorists. We also have to recognise that liberal democracies are bursting with political, social and moral conservatives – some in government, some in the media, some in educational institutions – who would like to turn the clock back on individual freedoms, particularly those inherited from the 60s. Sometimes, perhaps, they are right to defend traditions, standards and social cohesion. Sometimes, surely, they are wrong. But this much is absolutely clear: cyberterrorists and cyberpredators are endlessly invoked by those who seek to contain the explosion of online and offline freedoms, to limit the proliferation of new stories, and to bind individual and group narratives more closely to traditional societal narratives.

Education has always been political. At its best, it walks a tightrope between reproducing the status quo and providing open democratic spaces for challenging it. When teaching *through* digital technologies, educators have a responsibility to help students explore the power of these new tools to craft individual and communal stories, but also to help them perceive and compensate for their limitations and dangers. When teaching *about* digital technologies, educators have a responsibility to help students appraise the new tools through technological, pedagogical, social, sociopolitical and ecological lenses. Each lens will reveal different storytelling possibilities and different limitations. Taken together, these lenses can help both educators and students problematise the narrative freedoms offered by digital technologies, and simultaneously problematise the restrictions which some would like to impose on those freedoms. It's vital that today's students graduate with the creative skills to make the most of digital technologies, as well as the critical skills to evaluate the freedom or lack of freedom to which they may lead.

Digital technologies are set to play a major role in the future of education. Education must also play a major role in the future of digital technologies. The decisions we make today about education, technology, and technology in education must be informed by a consideration of the long-term social, sociopolitical and ecological consequences: in short, what kinds of stories – individual, local, national and global – they'll enable us to write. It's up to us to make sure we shape our technologies as much as they shape us. And, given the pace of ongoing technological development, we have to start now.

2

Many clouds

A technological lens

The first thing we see through a technological lens, metaphorically speaking, is clouds. Lots of them. For some, new technologies promise a future on cloud nine. Others spy threatening stormclouds on the horizon. Cloud computing, one of the defining developments of our time, captures something of both the promise and the threat. But mostly the lens is cloudy in quite another sense: because, despite having particular affordances, no technology determines how we use it. That part is up to us – and, for the moment, it's still unclear which way we're heading.

Cloud nine
Nowadays we hear a lot about the internet promoting individual autonomy, facilitating social connections and cultivating a sense of our common humanity. It's as if, in the new millennium, computers are reviving 1960s countercultural dreams of 'empowered individualism, collaborative community, and spiritual communion'.[1] Yet it's not a revival. The roots of today's personal, networked computing are planted firmly in the soil of the late 60s. The ideals of that time were there at its inception

and lay semi-dormant over the intervening decades while the net grew and developed, before maturing gradually into the connective structures of web 2.0.

Social liberation, then, was more than a backdrop to the origins of today's computing culture.[2] The outlook of many early designers and programmers was shaped by the hippie counterculture in whose heartland the 'mother of all demos'[3] took place in 1968, when Doug Engelbart publicly demonstrated networked computing – along with the mouse and hypertext – to a San Francisco audience. Notwithstanding the irony of its funding by the US military, the first electronic computer network, the ARPANET (Advanced Research Projects Agency Network), which later became the internet, was up and running by 1969. Intentionally designed as a robust, open network, largely for military reasons, it was structurally resistant to centralised control and tailored to lateral connections and cooperative interaction. It soon became a focal point for many who saw themselves as standing outside mainstream culture. In a later essay, 'We owe it all to the hippies', Stewart Brand put it this way: 'the counterculture's scorn for centralized authority provided the philosophical foundations of not only the leaderless Internet but also the entire personal-computer revolution'.[4] In fact, it's possible to trace a clear line running from Brand's *Whole Earth Catalog* (a kind of 'Google in paperback form'[5] which catered to the communes of the 1960s) via the WELL (the Whole Earth 'Lectronic Link virtual community which brought together the luminaries of 80s networked computing) to *Wired* magazine (the technoculture bible founded in 1993).[6] In spite of later commercial imperatives to make money, and political imperatives to staunch the free flow of information, something of this early ethos lives on.

In 1992, a year after the public release of Tim Berners-Lee's 'World Wide Web', which would eventually bring the benefits of networked computing to the masses, net pioneer David Clark perfectly captured the ongoing countercultural spirit: 'We reject: kings, presidents and voting', he said. 'We believe in: rough consensus and running code'.[7] Or as *Wired* cofounder Jane Metcalfe put it:

> The '60s generation had a lot of power, but they didn't have a lot of tools. And in many respects their protests were unable to implement long-term and radical change in our society. We do have the tools. The growth of the Internet and the growing political voice of the people on the Internet is proof of that.[8]

The same radically democratic spirit was echoed in *Time* magazine when, in recognition of the far-reaching impact of web 2.0, it announced 'You' as its Person of the Year in 2006. Beneath a cover picture of a computer, whose screen was a reflective panel in the print edition, it explained: 'You control the Information Age. Welcome to your world'.[9] Looking back over the past few decades, Charles Leadbeater observes that:

> the roots of the web-inflected culture we inhabit [are] a peculiar mixture of the academic, the hippie, the peasant and the geek. What binds them is a belief in the power of communities to share knowledge and other resources. Or to put it another way, the culture being created by the web is a potent mixture of post-industrial networks, the anti-industrial ideology of the counter-culture and the revival of pre-industrial ideas of organisation that were marginalised in the 20th century.[10]

In many ways, then, the post-millennial web 2.0 – some of whose individual tools have strong subcultural associations[11] – is a product of the 1960s.

Here's how it happened. Just as the ARPANET eventually gave us the internet, the internet eventually gave us the world wide web. The internet, essentially, is a network of computers connected around the globe. The web is a collection of interlinked documents which can be accessed through the internet. The net carries other services like email, instant messaging (IM) or online gaming, but the web is so overwhelmingly dominant in the popular imagination that 'web' and 'net' are often used interchangeably. In its original version, the web, now commonly called web 1.0, had an informational orientation, with a small number of authors producing material for a large number of users in the form of largely static webpages. It was like an electronic version of a reference book or a library. Educationally, therefore, it was suited to information transmission or behaviourist approaches: people could look things up (as in webquests) or do repetitive exercises (like drills or puzzles). While some educators soon began to make more inventive uses of the web and its growing store of multimedia materials, the inventiveness lay more in the design of the activities than in the web itself.

That changed with the advent of web 2.0, a term coined in 2004 by Dale Dougherty and popularised by Tim O'Reilly.[12] As O'Reilly has noted, in many ways 'the "2.0-ness" is not something new, but rather a fuller realization of the true potential of the web platform'.[13] With its 'architecture of participation',[14] web 2.0 is less like a thing (a book) or a place (a library) and more like a collaborative toolbox. It invites the 'people formerly known as the audience'[15] to find their voices and begin to turn monologues into dialogues and multi-logues. It offers every individual and every group the ability to speak and be heard, and to tell their story in their own words. This is made possible through a plethora of web 2.0 tools. If the web were a garden, web 1.0 tools would be imported plants from the land of books and libraries, while web 2.0 tools would be native plants, nurtured in local soil and much better adapted to the networked substrate. Most of these tools are freely available and, if not always fully 'open source' themselves, have philosophical roots in the open source movement which, with its emphasis on open, collaborative software design, draws heavily on the ethos of the early internet.

Web 2.0 includes tools like blogs, a kind of open diary (or magazine, or confessional, or tutorial) which anyone can publish, and where anyone else can comment, commiserate or argue. It includes wikis; that is, collaborative websites like Wikipedia, the online encyclopedia anyone can add to, edit or revise. It includes social networking sites like Facebook, MySpace, Bebo and Orkut, with their interlinked personal webpages where you can build an online presence as you interact with your social and professional networks; while if you want more creative control, you can form purpose-built networks with Ning. It includes social sharing sites like YouTube, where you can distribute and discuss videos you've recorded or remixed; Flickr and Photobucket, both primarily for photosharing; and SlideShare which, as the name suggests, is for sharing presentation slides. It includes social reviewing and rating sites, where you can publicise your assessments of everything from restaurants you've visited (Yelp) and concerts you've attended (Last.fm) to classes you've taken (RateMyProfessors.com); Amazon, eBay and iTunes all draw on this practice in different ways. It includes social news sites like Digg or Reddit, social advertising sites like craigslist, social decision-making sites like Hunch, and even social travel and accommodation sites like CouchSurfing. It includes microblogging services like Twitter, Plurk or Jaiku, which allow you to weave your own comments into the global conversational mesh. It includes services like Delicious for creating folksonomies, fuzzy indexing systems collaboratively generated by the 'folk' without reference to traditional top-down taxonomies. It includes community-driven social bookmarking and annotating services like Diigo, which lets you post notes on webpages and read those left by others. It includes really simple syndication (RSS) feeds which help you follow changes on sites you're interested in, allowing you to personalise your web environment to focus on what matters to you rather than what editors or experts think should matter. It includes self-published audio files called podcasts and video files called vodcasts, often syndicated via RSS, and the multimedia conversations to which these can lead. In short, web 2.0 is about a shift from what were primarily informational tools to what we might call relational tools[16] – so that, if web 1.0 was the *informational web*, web 2.0 is the *social web*. As a result, it has huge potential for educational approaches which centre not on transmission or repetition but on communication and collaboration.

But the web 2.0 explosion is far from over: new tools and services are appearing on a daily basis, while processes of convergence are seeing the spread of 'mashups', hybrid tools which combine functionality or data from different sources. Other net tools are also becoming more sophisticated. Voice over Internet Protocol (VoIP) software like Skype enables free internet telephony, while IM services, including web-based metaservices like Meebo, continue to proliferate. There are now over 300 virtual worlds,[17] the best known being Second Life, which allows people from all over the planet to interact through self-crafted 'avatars', or characters, in simulated three-dimensional environments. Massively multiplayer games like World of Warcraft connect role-playing individuals from around the globe as they pursue in-game goals. The hardware and infrastructure are becoming more sophisticated, too: the Japanese 'thumb tribe' of young SMS users has gone international with the spread of mobile phones – many of them now web- and GPS-enabled (that is, location-aware) – while governments are rolling out broadband networks and wireless hotspots are springing up in urban centres.

And the web itself is also continuing to evolve. Its next stage, web 3.0, is sometimes called the *semantic web*, in reference to Tim Berners-Lee's vision of software agents which will 'understand' the information on the web and draw on it to give 'intelligent' responses to human users. Others see web 3.0 as a *geospatial web* which will replace or supplement our current two-dimensional experience of webpages with a 3D environment, along the lines of a virtual world which we'll navigate with avatars. The future may hold some fusion of these two visions. Either way, it's unlikely web 3.0 will completely replace web 2.0, any more than web 2.0 replaced web 1.0; they'll co-exist, layered over each other, and people will choose when and how to access the informational web, the social web, the semantic web, or some combination of these.

Then again, predictions are risky. You never can tell what will emerge next from the 'wildly generative' combination of personal computers (PCs) and the internet which, by facilitating participatory input and innovative output,[18] has led to the current creative explosion. But neither can you tell when the generativity might end. For some, the generativity has already gone too far.

Stormclouds

When cartoonists and comedians begin to address a topic on a large scale, you know it's an area of real social concern. In recent years there's been a flood of ironic and satirical commentary on computers, the internet and the changes they're bringing about in society. One common focus is the speed of change. This anxiety is not misplaced. A 2008 report from the Australian Communications and Media Authority lists an 'accelerating pace of change' as the top technology trend of the next 5–10 years.[19] This naturally raises questions about the effects of rapid obsolescence and the cost of continual upgrades, all taking place amid a cloud of hype and speculation. Most of all, it raises the prospect of ongoing, radical instability.

When new software is developed, it typically goes through an 'alpha' stage of testing, followed by a 'beta' stage where it's released to users who are willing to try it out and provide feedback so bugs can be fixed. It's been noted by Tim O'Reilly (of 'web 2.0' fame) that we're now seeing the emergence of 'the perpetual beta' where products are effectively developed in the open, with users acting as co-developers and new fixes and features being released on a rolling basis.[20] It's a perfect fit for a

"I wouldn't say my computer skills are outdated. I prefer to think of them as 'classic'."

Figure 2.1. The speed of change. Cartoon © Randy Glasbergen, 2003, <www.glasbergen.com>.

web 2.0 world. But this new paradigm of endless, accelerated change is too much for many people, who are threatened by viruses, annoyed by bugs and driven to distraction by spam. (And that's before we get anywhere near cyberporn or cyberterror, issues we'll come back to later.) What's more, accelerated change doesn't just apply to technology. In some ways, as the cartoonists remind us, it's about technological changes least of all. In their wake come educational, social and political changes, many of which are also rapid and ongoing. Effectively, our whole culture has moved into perpetual beta, where changes happen so quickly, and are contributed to by so many diverse people and groups, that everything becomes provisional. There's real potential here for doing things a new way. But there are also lots of people, from parents to politicians and despots to democrats, who find their worldviews unsettled. And so, for both technological and sociopolitical reasons, there's a looming backlash against technology and the perpetual beta into which it's led us.

The dangers and distractions in the technology are real. There are those who want to protect themselves and their families, students, employees, customers or citizens. And there are those who have broader political, social or commercial agendas. Motives are muddied. But the end result is a clampdown on 'generativity', which Jonathan Zittrain defines as 'a system's capacity to produce unanticipated change through unfiltered contributions from broad and varied audiences'.[21] The open architecture of the net itself is under threat as (some) governments and (some) companies seek to regulate and police it. We're seeing the growing lockdown of PCs in offices and schools. We're seeing the rise of 'trusted computing', where users swap control for security on their own PCs. We're seeing the spread of devices like digital recorders and games consoles which, unlike programmable PCs, are non-generative (you can't program or alter them) and often tethered (and can thus be remotely manipulated or disabled by vendors long after they've been purchased).[22] We're seeing the advent of hybrid devices like the iPhone, where outside code can run but only once it's officially approved.[23] We're seeing the web increasingly filled with walled gardens in the form of password-protected virtual learning environments (VLEs) and social networking sites. Some of these developments, especially the last few, create safe and appealing environments – but ones with limited generativity. The danger is that the openness which brought us web 2.0 will be traded off against security, bringing the current wave of digital innovation to a shuddering halt.

We're also seeing a major shift towards 'cloud computing', in which your programs and data will no longer reside on your individual computer but, effectively, in cyberspace. Common cloud computing services already in wide use include webmail (such as Hotmail or Gmail), media storage services like Flickr and YouTube, and applications like Google Docs or Adobe Photoshop Express. Powered by Amazon's, Google's or IBM's cloud computing banks, computing will increasingly become, like electricity, a utility.[24] There are lots of advantages: it'll be low-maintenance, with PCs being no more than 'thin' devices that allow you to interface with the net, and software upgrades being handled centrally. It'll be cheaper, levelling the playing field for individuals and small businesses. It'll be flexible, as you'll be able to access any of your documents from anywhere and share them easily. However, there are serious disadvantages hovering on the horizon. On the one hand, there are limitations on generativity. On the other, there are limitations on your ability to control your own data, leading to privacy and security concerns. And this is only the start, as the virtual and the real blur together more and more…

Getting real

We don't see the radio or television as representing alternative realities except in a metaphorical sense. We don't see the telephone as a door to another universe. They're just entertainment and communication tools that enhance our everyday lives. Why, then, do we insist on seeing the internet as a 'virtual' space separated from the 'real' world? Perhaps it's partly a matter of degree. Perhaps it's a lack of familiarity. Either way, it doesn't make much sense to the younger generation, or to a growing proportion of the broader population, for whom life online is just an extension of (rather than qualitatively different from) life offline.

On the social networking site, Facebook, for example, analogue and digital networks intermesh as you marshal portraits of your online and offline friends alongside portraits of their Second Life avatars. You can pull together your snapshots from the photosharing service Flickr, your bookmarks from the folksonomy service Delicious, and your links to professional organisations, some of which may even 'meet' on Facebook. The same integrated channels you use for professional communication – like discussion board, webmail and IM features – can be used to make arrangements to catch up with friends, whether for an online Skype call or a couple of offline drinks. You can choose to learn a language virtually, with the help of an application like the *Japanese Audio Word of the Day*, and you can seek out online or offline language partners through the *Language Exchange*. You could be recruited to walk police dogs, help search for a missing person, or even join an intelligence agency – and if you're on the wrong side of the law you might find your court notice served through Facebook![25]

Can't make it down to your local library? Head for Info Island in Second Life. As with social networking sites, the line dividing virtual worlds from the 'real' one is becoming highly permeable. Banner-waving protests over the US in Iraq, and China in Tibet, have hit online islands at the same time as they hit offline streets. Barack Obama ran his Whitehouse campaign not only on Facebook and YouTube but in Second Life, while countries from the Maldives to Sweden have opened embassies there. The German virtual world Twinity is painstakingly digitising the streets of Berlin, with other cities to follow. Firms including Dell, IBM, Unilever and Xerox have held business meetings in virtual worlds, with Sun Microsystems drafting a rule that employees must turn up in human form![26] Hundreds of educational institutions, from the British Council to Edinburgh University, Harvard to Hong Kong Polytechnic University, and MIT to Monash have a presence in virtual worlds, most commonly Second Life. Meanwhile, as the law struggles to catch up with virtual crime, two Dutch teens have been convicted of stealing virtual goods.[27] Online infidelity has led to offline divorce, while a Japanese woman has been arrested after murdering the avatar of her online husband who had divorced her in an interactive game.[28] You can almost hear the ghost of postmodern philosopher Jean Baudrillard whispering from the wings: where does the simulation end? It doesn't. 'Real' and 'virtual' are two sides of the same coin.

And it's just a foretaste of what the emerging 'internet of things' will bring us. Radio-frequency identification (RFID) will soon make it possible to tag absolutely everything, animate or inanimate, and to

Figure 2.2. Tired of webpages? Try a book. Bell Library Tower, Info Island, Second Life. Image by Mark Pegrum, 2007. Used with permission of Lori Bell, Alliance Library System.

have every thing in communication with every other thing via the net. As a recent European Commission report puts it, it's about 'seamlessly integrating physical things into information networks'.[29] Yes, it means what it says: we're not far away from the day when you'll be able to Google your purse, your dog or your kid.[30] Convenient? Very. Worrying? Extremely. Already it's technologically possible to track all your online activity. Soon it may not matter much whether you're online or off. With classic understatement, the European Commission advises that there will be 'new challenges in protecting privacy and data'.[31]

For sure, it'll be a whole new world at the interface of the 'virtual' and the 'real' – filled with new educational, social and political promise, but dogged with very old human problems.

What's normal?

Historical blindness leads observers into two fundamental fallacies with respect to technology. The first is the fallacy of *technological determinism*: assuming that our technologies have the power to independently shape society, for good or ill. It's common among both techno-enthusiasts and techno-sceptics. Secondly, there's the opposite fallacy of *social determinism*: assuming that technologies themselves matter little and remain completely under our social control. It's particularly common among those who want to regulate the internet as if it were a TV station. The reality lies somewhere between these two poles. All technologies have particular 'affordances' that encourage you to do certain things with them rather than others. You can use a pen as a bookmark, but you're likely to use it more often to write. You can use a car to sleep in, but you're likely to use it more often to transport you places. But like pens and cars, no technology forces you to use it in particular ways. You can always choose to repurpose it – and even to use it against the grain, ignoring its original affordances or design. YouTube can be used to share remixed videos, but it can also be used as just another broadcast channel. Wikis can be an open collaboration platform, but they can also be controlled by a single editor. What we do with such technologies is, at least in part, up to us. In short, as we learned from Raymond Williams' work on television in the 70s, 'technology is both socially shaped and socially shaping'.[32]

There's a third fallacy, too, which we might call *exceptionalism*: assuming that new technologies are so unusual that they will always be considered, first and foremost, as 'Technologies'. History tells us, however, that in time all technologies become normalised. That is, we stop seeing them as technologies and start seeing them as tools which suit some purposes and not others. It's only when technologies become 'boring' in this way that their full potential can be realised.[33] Stephen Bax makes this point in respect of computer-assisted language learning (CALL), but it applies equally to all areas of education. Teachers, he says, must move beyond reactions of fear and awe and view computers as tools – like pens or whiteboards – which can be used in the service of given pedagogical goals.[34] danah boyd (yes, all lower case) makes the same point more broadly:

> [P]lease adult world, I beg you…stop fearing and/or fetishizing technology. Neither approach does us any good. Technology is not the devil, nor is it the panacea you've been waiting for. It's a tool. Just like a pencil. Figure out what it's good for and leverage that to your advantage.[35]

Naturally, it's difficult for still-emerging technologies to become normalised in the same way as more established ones.[36] However, we may need to acclimatise ourselves to a culture of perpetual beta where the very notion of emerging technologies becomes normalised, so that we can move much more quickly beyond paralysing and unproductive states of fear and fetishisation. This would allow us to experiment broadly and confidently with new tools as well as, crucially, reflecting on why and how we're using them. Until technology becomes normalised, there's typically too much focus on the technology itself and not enough on how it's used pedagogically, socially, politically or ecologically.

Andrew Feenberg, a prominent early commentator on electronic technologies in education, noted that technology is 'not a destiny but a scene of struggle'.[37] Technology today is a battlefield on which contests over different visions of society are still being fought out. The outcomes are not foretold. Ultimately, it's the breadth of our view of digital technologies, obtained through whichever lenses we use, that will determine what we will or won't make of these technologies; whether we'll work with or against their affordances; and what we'll allow them to become or not become. We have to go beyond a technological lens. We have to make use of pedagogical, social, sociopolitical and ecological lenses to better understand the bigger picture, and ensure that our technologies are bringing the greatest benefits to the greatest number of people.

Many literacies

A pedagogical lens

The Chennai exhortation to remember the three Ps of e-learning – pedagogy, pedagogy and pedagogy! – neatly captures the growing realisation that technology cannot be allowed to drive pedagogy. It suggests that the process of normalisation is already underway and that pedagogical concerns are beginning to take precedence over technological issues.

But there's a complication. As we've seen, technologies are not deterministic, even if they do have particular affordances. Digital technologies can be used in support of contemporary educational approaches, but they can also be used in support of much more traditional approaches. The contrasting possibilities have come to a head with web 2.0. Although, educationally speaking, web 1.0 opened up a few limited possibilities to do things differently, it's the affordances of web 2.0 that are bringing to fruition the revolutionary, liberalising promise of the internet. When educators work with those affordances, web 2.0 opens up spaces for constructivist, collaborative pedagogies. But if educators work against its grain, web 2.0 can be used narrowly as an electronic add-on to automate information transmission and skills practice. Many governments and more than a few teachers, parents and social commentators would like just that to happen.

As a result, we find ourselves in the midst of a sometimes savage struggle over the meaning of digital learning and digital literacy. And we have to remember that debates which appear to be about technology, or for that matter about education, often reflect deep-seated social beliefs and far-reaching political agendas. It's those beliefs and agendas which will ultimately determine whether, and to what extent, we'll teach with or against the affordances of web 2.0.

Web 2.0 in education

Western education is no longer preparing students to take their places in industrial economies organised around hierarchies, standardised roles and mass production.[1] Instead, it's preparing them for post-industrial – that is, post-Fordist or knowledge-based – economies, which demand autonomy, creativity, flexibility, collaboration and lifelong learning. One-off qualifications, standardised for the whole population, don't cut it in this new world. It's a world where '[t]he ability to draw on rote answers is inadequate' because 'yesterday's answers are outdated faster than ever'.[2] It's a world where, as stated in a 2006 report for the British Columbia Ministry of Advanced Education in Canada, conceptual thinking and problem solving will be vital skills.[3] It's a world where, as the 2008 Australia–New Zealand *Horizon Report* stresses, there is a workplace-driven need for 'hands-on, purpose-driven, authentic, and other active learning approaches'.[4] Both of these reports also focus on collaboration: it's becoming increasingly important to know how to seek out information through networks of contacts and to be able to cooperatively build understanding with others. In a similar vein, a 2008 CISCO report comments that 'traditional education systems fostered the obedience demanded of the manufacturing workforce' but new approaches are now needed to 'nurture creative and collaborative skills';[5] while in 2009, the Australian Industry Group, the Business Council of Australia and the Australian Chamber of Commerce and Industry called for universities to place more emphasis on students' skills of 'communication, teamwork and problem-solving'.[6] In short, there's a strong need for educational approaches which prepare students adequately for this changed, and changing, work landscape. Fortunately, help is at hand.

Social constructivism is a key pedagogical approach of our time. Despite its origins in the work of Soviet psychologist Lev Vygotsky in the 1930s, and despite certain parallels with John Dewey's progressivism from the first half of the twentieth century, it didn't come to prominence in the West until late in the twentieth century. As a philosophy, it rejects the notion that reality is objectively knowable, suggesting rather that we construct our own mental representations of it according to input, experience and interaction with others. As a pedagogical approach, it departs from traditional transmission models: those that see the teacher's role as transmitting an objective body of knowledge to largely passive students who arrive in class as 'blank slates'. It also departs from behaviourist models: those which emphasise learning and mastery through repetition. Constructivism puts learners, rather than a given body of knowledge, at the centre of the learning process, and aims to build on the pre-existing knowledge and perspectives they bring into the classroom. As students actively engage in educational experiences based on authentic tasks, with guidance provided by teachers or more experienced peers, they collaboratively build new understandings. Facilitated by competent teachers, this can be an empowering strategy that encourages the sharing of ideas, giving everyone a voice without unnecessarily imposing particular points of view. There's little doubt that such an approach is demanding and time-consuming for both educators and students, but it offers considerable rewards in terms of subtlety and complexity. At its best, it leads to the development of autonomy, flexibility and strategies for cooperation, collaboration and negotiation.[7] As such, social constructivism – along with related approaches and frameworks like inquiry-based learning, problem-based learning, communities of practice and connectivism – is ideally suited to preparing students for a post-industrial context.

In turn, web 2.0's dialogue building and social networking tools, themselves a subset of the digital tools on which post-industrial economies depend, provide an ideal vehicle for social constructivism, offering 'a means whereby just about anyone can contribute to an ongoing "conversation" in which knowledge is both discovered and constructed as it goes on'.[8] In this way, web 2.0, which has helped change the ground rules about 'who gets to say what to whom',[9] lends something of its post-60s ethos to the ongoing educational revolt against older transmission and behaviourist approaches (though whether new pedagogies can or should entirely replace older ones is a complex question to which we'll return).

Web 2.0 tools are flexible, too. They can be used within an *e-learning* framework involving fully online instruction. More commonly, they are used within a *blended learning* framework combining face-to-face and online instruction to maximise the benefits of both. They can even be used within an *m-learning* (mobile learning) framework involving mobile computing devices deployed in everyday contexts. Whatever the framework, students can coordinate their online experiences through 'e-portfolios' or 'personal learning environments' (PLEs). These are individually tailored constructivist spaces built by and for learners. They may take the form of websites, blogs, wikis, social networking pages or some hybrid of these. Learners are able to draw on the full gamut of web 2.0 tools as they use these spaces to assemble their individual and collaborative work, most likely in multiple media, and crystallise their networks of connections to people and communities from across the web. While PLEs typically have a learning focus, e-portfolios may also serve display purposes: your e-portfolio, in other words, can become your CV. PLEs and e-portfolios, in short, provide a framework within which social constructivism and web 2.0 can function in a remarkably productive combination.

And constructivism and web 2.0, together, can go a long way to preparing students for the digitally driven, post-industrial world into which they'll graduate – a world where our understandings of knowledge, culture, truth and authority are in the process of being rewritten.

Knowledge is collaborative

In 2008, students taking exams at Presbyterian Ladies' College in Sydney were allowed to use the internet or iPods and even 'phone a friend' on their mobiles, as the school responded to a challenge from Marc Prensky (who coined the term 'digital natives') to regard such activities not as cheating, but as 'using our tools and including the world in our knowledge base'. As the Dean of Years 7 to 9 explained:

> In their working lives [the students] will never need to carry enormous amounts of information around in their heads. What they will need to do is access information from all their sources quickly and they will need to check the reliability of their information.[10]

In a digital world, knowledge is, less than ever, an individual possession. It's a property of the network. 'Cheating', therefore, becomes a normal strategy. What counts is the ability to access, evaluate, collate and synthesise information from a variety of contacts and sources, and contribute to it yourself – whether in a minor way (by adding or editing details) or a major way (by developing original insights). As David Weinberger puts it: 'knowledge isn't in our heads: It is between us'.[11] Digital tools give us unprecedented opportunities to link up this distributed intelligence, harnessing it in a form known as 'collective intelligence'. Collective intelligence is shared rather than individual, and collaborative rather than competitive. It takes two main forms which, though they're often confused with each other and may sometimes even overlap, are distinct.

Firstly, there's what James Surowiecki has famously described as the 'wisdom of crowds', based on the aggregation of diverse independent decisions.[12] It's at work in the 'crowdsourcing' of decisions on the importance of webpages which underpins the PageRank algorithm that drives Google. In simplified form, a link by webpage B to webpage A is regarded as a 'vote', whose value is determined by how many other webpages have in turn linked to webpage B, and so on. Each 'vote' is made independently without 'voters' directly influencing each other. The aggregated results constitute the wisdom of the crowd, which is generally 'smarter' than any given individual, and determine the order of results returned in a Google search.[13] The wisdom of crowds is also at work in the popular voting on social news services like Digg or Reddit. It's there, too, in the organic indexing processes which underpin folksonomies, with their collections of 'tags' (descriptive terms added to webpages by users) presented as spatially organised 'tag clouds'. Educators are already beginning to exploit the potential for 'collaborative

Figure 3.1. Learning by 'cheating'. Chris Surridge's avatar, Christopher Flow, talks on 'Motivated Interactions in Second Life' at the SLanguages 2008 Conference, EduNation, Second Life, 23–24 May.
Image by Mark Pegrum, 2008. Used with permission of Chris Surridge & Gavin Dudeney.

information discovery'[14] which emerges as students cooperatively construct class folksonomies through services like Delicious. However, when teachers introduce a negotiated element into class exercises, they are starting to move in the direction of a second kind of collective intelligence.

This second notion of collective intelligence, derived from the work of Pierre Lévy and championed by Henry Jenkins, is more often what people have in mind when they use the term to talk about web 2.0. It depends on purposeful engagement, argument and consensus building.[15] Early evidence of its power can be seen in the open source movement which, through unpaid, voluntary contributions, has produced powerful, stable resources like the Apache software used by many web servers, the Linux operating system, the Mozilla Firefox browser, and the Moodle and Sakai VLEs. But it's web 2.0 tools like wikis which most obviously turn this sort of collective intelligence into a structural principle. Wikis invite participation by anyone with information, knowledge or perspectives to share. Typically regulated by a community of users, they are safeguarded by a standardised history function which allows past page versions to be recovered in case of vandalism or disputes over content. Despite a small number of widely publicised cases of vandalism or inaccuracy, the web 2.0 prodigy, Wikipedia, has proven to be almost as accurate as *Encyclopaedia Britannica*[16] – and, with 2.95 million articles in English alone as of mid-July 2009, it's far more comprehensive and up-to-date. Educators are now successfully using wikis as forums where students can draft and redraft work collaboratively, building on and modifying each other's contributions in the light of feedback from peers, teachers or, on public wikis, the entire internet.

If intelligence is collective and knowledge is collaborative, the traditional educational emphasis on individual regurgitation of memorised facts must cede space to newer pedagogies and assessments. Certainly, today's students need to learn to cooperate with one another at least as much as they need to learn to compete.

Culture is participatory

Not long after September 11, TV stations around the Western world broadcast an odd spectacle: Bangladeshi protestors were seen marching through the streets waving placards showing Osama bin Laden – and, in the background, an image of Bert from the *Sesame Street* duo, Bert and Ernie. A photoshopped image created by a US high school student, Dino Ignacio, it had been unwittingly copied by Bangladeshis, leading to a collision of symbols of a kind which is becoming more and more common thanks to the spread of digital technologies.[17] No longer is media production solely in the hands of large corporations; it's finding its way into the hands of ordinary citizens.

In digital culture, we're seeing a proliferation of 'user-generated content' (UGC), especially and most dramatically in the form of 'remixes' (sometimes also referred to as 'mashups', the same term used for hybrid computer applications). These combine pre-existing video, images, music and/or text to create new hybrids. It's a return to traditional folk creativity after the industrial hiatus of the twentieth century, which gave us spectacular cultural products but at the price of making much of humanity passive recipients rather than active producers of culture. After all, prior to the advent of mass reproduction, most culture *was* user-generated.[18] Several decades ago, Alvin Toffler anticipated the rise of the 'prosumer' (producer/consumer) but, writing in a contemporary context, Axel Bruns prefers the term 'produser' (producer/user), which avoids the industrial and commercial implications of Toffler's coinage.[19] Bruns' term highlights the fact that the distinction is once again narrowing between producers and users of content. And it's not just kids at play, either. We're facing what Charles Leadbeater and Paul Miller term a 'pro-am' (professional/amateur) revolution, where more and more people are 'pursuing amateur activities to professional standards'.[20] Kids' playful experiments feed into this pro-am culture as they hone their knowledge and skills in their chosen areas of creativity. And the kids are getting more creative: in 2004, 57 per cent of 12 to 17-year-olds in the US had created online content, a figure which rose to 64 per cent by 2006.[21]

There are countless ways of getting involved in this culture, many of which young people have already taken up – and many of which can be exploited in education. Blogs and moblogs (mobile blogs) can help students shape and share their thoughts while learning from feedback: contrary to common perceptions, blogs are rarely about 'diarism in isolation' but involve connecting your thoughts to wider events and others' commentary on them.[22] Students can submit academic work to Wikipedia (where they can receive feedback through others' subsequent edits) and creative work to Flickr (where feedback may take the form of comments) or YouTube (where responses may range from textual discussion to video replies). They can even build a 'sim' (virtual location) in Second Life, like the Melbourne 2051 student project, and open it for public inspection. In many cases, students can opt to waive copyright on individually created pieces, distributing them under Creative Commons (CC) licences and thus adding their work to the more than 150 million pieces in the digital commons which have been licensed this way since the launch of CC licences in 2002. Finally, any individual student's creations and contributions can be linked together through a PLE and can even form the basis for an e-portfolio, with blogs, wiki entries, Flickr photos, YouTube videos and Second Life constructions shaped into a digital CV.

But UGC is about more than creativity for educational or job-seeking purposes. The rise of what Henry Jenkins calls 'participatory culture' means ever greater involvement in national and international conversations by ever larger numbers of people. This opens up the potential for a 'semiotic democracy',[23] as William Fisher calls it, where the broader population becomes involved in contributing to the stories we tell of our own times. If, as critics claim, this vastly increases the potential for ill-considered and banal commentary, it also vastly increases the potential for informed and subtle commentary. There is much educators can do to promote the latter as they help students to capitalise on their digital opportunities:

> Politics, as constructed by the news, becomes a spectator sport, something we watch but do not do. Yet, the new participatory culture offers many opportunities for youth to engage in civic debates, to participate in community life, to become political leaders [...][24]

Some of this engagement may take the form of traditional political commentary through new forums like blogs, or traditional civic organising through new channels like social networking sites. But much of it is likely to take the form of multimedia remixes, which have their own logic and require their own literacy to decode, as we'll see. They may also lead to copyright complications, an issue educators need to consider when they venture into this territory with their students. This much is certain, though: all of us are going to have to get used to Bert marching with bin Laden.

Truth is provisional

Amid the collapse of Marxist utopianism in 1960s Paris, a philosophical movement took shape which insisted that the modernists, with their confident plans to improve the world through Enlightenment rationalism, had got it very, very wrong. Later, it was dubbed *post*modernism. Its most enduring value has perhaps been its relentless, deconstructive questioning, which undermines familiar certainties about knowledge, truth and authority. As another child of the 60s, something of its ethos has found its way into web 2.0, which elevates provisionality to a governing principle.

User tagging leads us away from the rigid, ethnocentric taxonomies of an era when knowledge seemed finite, and towards a fluid, evolving classification system or set of systems for an infinitely expandable knowledge space.[25] Facebook and MySpace updates are ephemeral snapshots of what's important one moment, but may not be the next. Blog entries are temporary formulations of your latest thoughts, subject to revision at any moment within the ongoing conversations of the blogosphere. Wiki pages can be amended or rewritten by anyone, anytime. Writers have caught on to this trend and increasingly use blogs and wikis to open up their work to commentary: as a friend remarked to Charles Leadbeater when he was about to post the first draft of *We-Think* online, it's less about writing a book and more about having a conversation.[26] Similarly, blogs are turning journalism into more of a conversation. Twitter is doing much the same for public presentations, with many speakers finding that audiences are using their mobile phones to 'tweet' (that is, post) comments and questions, confer with one another, and relay summaries to those not present; more adventurous speakers are even beginning to shape their talks around this real-time audience feedback.

It's been suggested that the outcomes of web 2.0-enabled collaborative projects are 'the polar opposites of [...] products: they are inherently incomplete, always evolving, modular, networked, and never finished'.[27] Arguably Wikipedia's greatest contribution to our culture has been to show that knowledge, far from being eternal and sacrosanct, is subject to (re-)editing at any time. It lays bare the constructed nature of truth, as Cory Doctorow explains:

> What's most fascinating about these entries isn't their 'final' text as currently present on Wikipedia. It is the history page for each, blow-by-blow revision lists that make it utterly transparent where the bodies were buried on the way to arriving at whatever Truth has emerged. This is a neat solution to the problem of authority [...][28]

A wiki is social constructivism in motion: collaboratively constructed, constantly added to and modified, and always provisional. The collective intelligence which emerges from contributors' cooperative efforts is never fixed but constantly evolving. Maybe, suggests Cass Sunstein, a wiki is a good model for the state of human knowledge.[29] And maybe, as a result, there's a lot for students to learn as they work with wikis and other similar web 2.0 tools, not just about the results of their particular projects, but about the mechanisms for constructing truth itself.

Authority is distributed

In 2008, the Sydney Powerhouse Museum became the first museum in the world to release its historical images on the Flickr photosharing site. It's one small part of a broad trend for more and more information to become available digitally, thanks to initiatives as diverse as the Google Books Library Project, the Internet Archive, the Open Content Alliance or UNESCO's World Digital Library. But it's not just old material. Present-day cultural creations with CC licences circulate rapidly on the web. News is accessible as it breaks, often from multiple sources. Up-to-date knowledge vetted by experts can be found in the online Encyclopedia of Life or Medpedia. In protest against expensive, locked down journals, some academics are publishing in open access journals, while a number of institutions now encourage or even require staff to make their research openly available.[30] In a clear assault on proprietary models, many universities offer lecture podcasts free of charge on iTunes U, while the Open Educational Resources movement freely gives away vast amounts of course material through initiatives like MIT's OpenCourseWare and the OU's OpenLearn.

We're moving rapidly from a paradigm of scarcity to one of abundance, where access to information, knowledge and culture is

Figure 3.2. Nineteenth century Sydney meets the twenty-first century. Circular Quay, Sydney, 1892.
From the Powerhouse Museum Collection of copyright-free images on Flickr.

being democratised (as is participation in information, knowledge and cultural creation, as we've seen). Nevertheless, predictions of the demise of informational and cultural mediators are much exaggerated. Democratised access doesn't mean we no longer need experts but that we need their expertise in a different way: not as gatekeepers but as facilitators and explicators. Awash in a sea of UGC, we need, more than ever, the information seeking and classifying skills of librarians, the trained and informed perspectives of critics, the investigative and analytic resources of journalists, and the guiding and mentoring talents of teachers.

What's different, though, is that no one is obliged to accept the versions of reality presented to them by these or any other experts. Anyone can challenge their librarians, their critics, their journalists and their teachers. Students can pick their own teachers to follow on Twitter, apprenticing themselves to communities of practice of their choice. Bloggers can act as 'a global fact-checking posse', exposing false news stories reported in the mainstream media.[31] Cultural aficionados can add their own reviews to movie websites, or contribute their own playlists to online radio stations. Users of all kinds of information can add value to it: by tagging, commenting on, and even modifying or correcting it. That's why Lynne Brindley, Chief Executive of the British Library, says the future relationship between librarians and patrons will be more like one of equals, built on user participation and the facilitation of communities of practice around digital content.[32]

If information, knowledge and culture are increasingly pervasive, participatory and provisional, they can't be easily managed, much less guaranteed, by gods or governments. Authority is more broadly distributed. That's not the same as saying authority disappears: it's been widely noted, for example, that many open source and open access projects, from Linux to Wikipedia, layer a kind of benevolent dictatorship over the networked interactions at their core. But this new kind of authority is earned rather than imposed and is contingent on ongoing community acceptance. As *Wall Street Journal* blogger Gary Hamel puts it: 'On the Web, authority trickles up, not down'.[33]

Where does this leave classroom teachers? Their authority, too, is reduced or at least opened to scrutiny in a sometimes uncomfortable way. They can no longer act as oracles, if indeed they ever really could: they need to earn the respect of their students. Yet they're more important than ever as facilitators of student learning. Students need experienced guides to help them find, analyse and synthesise information; contribute to common knowledge; grasp changing cultural patterns; and start to shape the culture around them. Who is better placed than teachers to coach students in the many literacies they'll need to make sense of, and participate effectively in, the new digital culture?

Many literacies

In a post-industrial context, literacy plays a pivotal role. It's not only about the limited functional literacy (say, form filling or list writing) which seemed sufficient for most people in industrial economies, but about much more complex uses of language. And it's not only about standardised, monolingual print literacy, but about literacy in a diverse range of media and cultural frameworks. While the following discussion isn't meant to generate an inventory of literacies to be ticked off by teachers or students, it's important to think about some of the skillsets necessary to engage effectively in contemporary communication.

Print literacy

First up, there's *print literacy*, which is, after all, still a key literacy. Subsuming spelling, grammar and discourse, and often associated with extended prose, it has far more than historical value. Reading long texts may be the best way to cultivate deep reflection or incisive questioning. Writing long texts may be the best way to establish conceptual frameworks or make persuasive arguments. Books, especially, are important vehicles for transmitting 'a fully fledged worldview'.[34] That's why I see no contradiction in writing a book like this about digital technologies, and that's why the Select Bibliography consists of books, with their sustained arguments, alongside the topical conversations of blogs and the swift salvos of microblogs. Nor are books inimical to digital culture, as the sheer number of bookshops and libraries in Second Life shows! To deprive students of the chance to immerse themselves in the contemplative texts of our modernist tradition (away from blinking cursors and beckoning hyperlinks) or to develop the skills to express themselves precisely in extended prose (even if that's with the aid of cursors and hyperlinks) would be to seriously impoverish their education – not to mention their later job options.

Search literacy

Most online experiences start at Google (the world's dominant search engine), YouTube (in second place as of late 2008) and other common search engines or portals like Yahoo!, Microsoft's Bing, Baidu (in China) or Naver (in South Korea). Searching, according to Google CEO Eric Schmidt, 'is empowering for humans like nothing else. It is the antithesis of being told or taught. It is about self-empowerment'.[35] Be that as it may, there are traps. Many students don't realise that different search engines return different results, or that multi-word queries return different results from single-word queries. Many don't understand the role of commerce in commercial search engines. Many don't think about who might get left out of Google's 'worldwide popularity contest',[36] where the 'wisdom of crowds' which underpins search rankings may let down those minorities, dissenters or nonconformists who aren't part of the main crowd. Many are completely unaware that search engines record and aggregate users' activities. In short, there's a pressing need for *search literacy*.

A subcategory of search literacy, *tagging literacy*, is essential to make the most of folksonomies. Students must understand their advantages (flexibility, extensibility) and limitations (vagueness, inconsistency), learning how to read them with and against traditional taxonomies. Having stepped outside the ethnocentric boundaries of the Dewey Decimal Classification System, they'll need to consider the impact of diverse social and cultural perspectives on the language used for tagging and how that, in turn, might impact the usability of tags in a global context. With sufficient training and experience, they can become reflective and cooperative taggers in their own right, contributing their own perspectives and insights to others' future searches.

Information literacy

Online materials shouldn't be approached as if they were print materials. 'Reading Wikipedia like *Britannica* stinks', says Cory Doctorow. 'Reading Wikipedia like Wikipedia is mind-opening.'[37] Students have to learn how to read the multivoiced, provisional, evolving documents of digital culture, which aren't designed to be read in the same way as the edited, finished, stable products of analogue culture. They also need to be aware of the very real danger of what Stephen Colbert calls 'wikiality': 'a reality where, if enough people agree with a notion, it must be true'[38]... another downside of collective intelligence. (It's not just wikis: similar issues exist with blogs and other digital documents.[39]) Thus, students need to develop the *information literacy* – or *critical literacy* – skills to evaluate the origins, authorship, history, accuracy, objectivity, completeness, currency and relevance of digital documents, and to compare and cross-reference them with other digital as well as analogue sources. There are no quick fixes: it'll be a long, painstaking learning process, with multiple failures littering the road to competence. On a macro level, information literacy must be supplemented by *filtering literacy*, the ability to quickly sift through a multitude of sources, ideally supported by the ability to choose the most appropriate informational mediators – librarians, critics or journalists – to turn to in any given context. At the same time, it is important to develop *network literacy*; that is, the ability to leverage social and professional networks to keep abreast of key information and access specific information as required. On a micro level, information literacy must be supplemented by *hypertext literacy*, involving an ability to understand the rhetorical effects of links (how they subtly affect a document's emphases, balance, openness and credibility) and to respond to their navigational effects (as they empower, or force, readers to actively build their own narrative trails across multiple documents).

Undoubtedly, it's useful for students to acquire basic factual histories and geographies of their own societies and fields of study to give them a sense of rootedness and help contextualise their understanding of new information. But in a world where information can and will be Googled in an instant, it's clear that rote memorisation has to yield some prominence to search literacy (including tagging literacy) and information literacy (including filtering and hypertext literacy). Yes, there's plenty of misinformation and disinformation on the net, but that's precisely why students need to learn, early on, how to navigate through it. If schools mandate filters or, worse still, if teachers themselves act as filters by vetting all digital material, we deny students some of the most important lessons of the digital age. Approached sensibly, Google and Wikipedia may be the two most useful educational sites on the net, not just because of the information they give us access to, but because of the lessons they teach about search and information literacy.

Participatory literacy
In digital culture, readers are also writers. They add value involuntarily to search data and voluntarily to folksonomies. It's in the nature of *participatory literacy* that they can also contribute in a host of different ways to blogs, wikis, social networking and sharing sites, virtual worlds and even gaming environments.

It's true that there are specialised fields where the non-initiated may have little to add, but there are many others where contributions from a wide range of users can feed into collective intelligence: a notion lent weight by the fact that even *Britannica* has moved towards a hybrid model allowing vetted user contributions.[40] Conversely, over the past few years Wikipedia has introduced certain levels of protection to preserve the quality of its articles, particularly biographies of the living.[41] Recently, in the wake of the premature announcement in January 2009 of Edward Kennedy's death, consideration was given to a possible need for editorial approval of any changes to such biographies.[42] Could a combination of wide collaboration plus limited expert intervention – community creation with benevolent oversight – become the pattern of future knowledge development? If so, it's already being modelled in educational institutions around the world, as teachers offer feedback on work which their students post, individually or collaboratively, on public wikis, or encourage students to draw on work that's already been marked as they contribute to sites like Wikipedia.

Digital literacy, in sum, is less passive than print literacy and demands that engaged citizens continually add to, challenge and modify online documents. Yet that in turn requires an extension of skills normally associated with the print literacy era, namely building coherent arguments and engaging in sustained discussions, which may be necessary to persuasively carry a point on a blog or a wiki. Similarly, many such forums retain strict requirements regarding plagiarism. Teachers may need to clarify the sometimes subtle distinction between copying and collaborating; to emphasise the importance of intellectual honesty in referencing sources; and to stress that the rules of attribution operating on blogs and wikis (as in most print contexts) differ from those of the broader digital culture of borrowing and remixing, where attribution, if it exists, is typically implicit rather than explicit.

Beyond plagiarism and the resulting copyright issues, it's important to avoid giving students a utopian impression of participatory literacy. In part, this is because clashes and confrontations are built into what we might call the 'wiki model' of arriving at a consensus, which distils and amplifies the kinds of conflicts inherent in most rational debate. As Clay Shirky points out, for example, Wikipedia 'is the product not of collectivism but of unending argumentation',[43] while the man at the helm of Wikipedia, Jimmy Wales, puts it this way: 'We need to have places on the internet […] to *disagree* with each other *safely* [emphasis added]'. [44] Both parts of his statement are important: the safety, and the disagreement. But more than this, as Andrew Lih has noted in regard to Wikipedia, there can be an 'unsavory agonistic' aspect – indeed, we could say a wilfully antagonistic aspect – to online interactions.[45] Dealing with constant challenges and criticisms may be difficult enough, but dealing with 'trolls', 'flamers' and vandals requires real psychological robustness. The darker side of online interaction is equally found in other internet forums, from social networking sites to virtual worlds, meaning that personal digital safety must also be a core consideration, a point we'll explore in more detail in the next chapter.

Multiliteracies

Members of the New Literacy Studies movement and the New London Group have long argued for a greater recognition of multiple literacies, or *multiliteracies*,[46] some of which have taken on a new salience in the digital age. *Visual literacy* is central to a global culture in which graphics and iconography are rising in importance vis-à-vis text.[47] It's crucial to interpreting webpages, tag clouds, and the results in visual search engines like Grokker, Quintura or TagGalaxy, and it plays a role in composing many kinds of online messages. *Audio literacy* and *video literacy* are growing in importance thanks to the explosion of podcasts and vodcasts, not to mention political and social commentary circulating virally in the form of songs or videos. *Media literacy*, focusing on critical analysis of traditional media, is as relevant as ever, with commercial productions becoming more accessible through online channels and embedded advertising becoming ubiquitous. Most commonly, what's needed is *multimodal literacy*, with digital technologies typically demanding competence in a range of the above literacies, including the ability to shift between different clusters of literacies as required. We could even make a case for *virtual world literacy* or *gaming literacy*, incorporating and building on specific kinds of multimodal and participatory literacy.

Remix literacy

In 2001, as we've seen, Bert went marching with bin Laden. In 2003, the Bush–Blair love song, an anti-Iraq protest, went viral: a video created by Swedish director Johan Söderberg, it spliced together news footage of Tony Blair and George Bush in such a way that the two leaders appeared to be professing their love for one another as they lip-synched to the Lionel Richie and Diana Ross duet, 'Endless Love', with Blair in the female role. In 2008, young Australians flooded the net with parodies of the Rudd Government's net censorship proposals: the Prime Minister's image was photoshopped onto Chairman Mao's *Little Red Book* and transplanted into *Big Brother* posters, and he was even given a starring role in a *South Park* clip. Encoding and decoding the sophisticated messages in these works – whether videos, to which the term 'remix' is most commonly applied, or still images – requires *remix literacy*, one of the hallmarks of the digital age.

Because it blends together others' work, any given remix is effectively the product of many individuals, so that, as Dan Perkel observes, remixing may be seen 'as a sign of a new, *networked material intelligence* [emphasis in original]'[48] – a kind of collective intelligence. Remixed UGC is about the originality of the juxtapositions, the irony of the contrasts and the power of the message which is conveyed to others who are literate in this medium. It's emerging as a core part of the political and civic discourse of the younger generation. As Lawrence Lessig points out:

> It is now anybody with access to a $1500 computer who can take sounds and images from the culture around us and use it to say things differently. [...] It is a literacy for this generation. This is how our kids speak. It is how our kids think. It is what your kids are [...][49]

Henry Jenkins, speaking of still images, calls it 'Photoshop for democracy – where participatory culture becomes participatory government'.[50] Of course, this parodic politics is a long way from traditional political or civil engagement. Colin Lankshear and Michele Knobel see it as a new *meme literacy*, where memes are defined as 'contagious patterns of cultural information that [...] directly shape and propagate key actions and mindsets of a social group'. The remixes which help spread these memes, they suggest, have more to do with 'being smart than being truthful, correct, or proficient in conventional terms'.[51] Sometimes the point is very clear, as in the Bush–Blair love song or the Rudd photomontages. Sometimes the point may simply be to relativise the truth claims of pre-existing texts or images in postmodern style: Bert meets bin Laden.

The kids are already photoshopping bin Laden, Bush and Rudd. Wouldn't it be good for educators to engage more fully with this energy and creativity? Howard Rheingold puts it this way:

> [W]e have an opportunity today to make use of the natural enthusiasm of today's young digital natives for cultural production as well as consumption, to help them learn to use the media production and distribution technologies now available to them to develop a public voice about issues they care about.[52]

At the same time, it would be helpful for educators to discuss with students the effectiveness of this mode of expression, including whether and how it might be complemented by the use of more conventional channels and literacies, and when and why it might lead to copyright issues. There's no doubt, though, that remix literacy is here to stay and is already having a major impact on how young people participate in the making of our culture.

Personal literacy

For the younger generation in particular, identity is mediated by digital technology. R.W. Burniske suggests that educators must help students acquire *personal literacy*; that is, an understanding of how to present themselves and how others will 'read' them on the web.[53] It's a macro-literacy which draws on elements of traditional literacy like language and discourse control alongside newer digital literacies. 'Within cyberspace', says Tina Kazan, 'writers have flexibility in how they construct a self and the more strategies they acquire, the more flexibility they have'.[54] The role of educators is to ensure students' choices are not limited by a narrow exposure to print literacy, but that they can 'make informed rhetorical choices' grounded in an easy familiarity with the many literacy practices at their disposal, as they tell their own digital stories through their blogs, microblogs, wikis, social networking and social sharing sites.

Intercultural literacy

Many of the new literacies involve a strong interpersonal communicative element; indeed, Mark Warschauer has written specifically of *computer-mediated communication (CMC) literacy*, which is relevant to interactive discourse involving tools ranging from email to discussion boards and contexts ranging from the social to the academic.[55] Certainly, in a world of multidirectional communication, it's crucial to develop digital *communicative literacy*, which provides a foundation for online interactions, based in netiquette and negotiating strategies, and facilitates the collaborative processes at the core of participatory literacy. And in a world where diverse cultures rub together in electronic networks, it's essential for students to simultaneously acquire the *cultural literacy* which will allow them to read artefacts, from print texts to multimedia remixes, produced in a range of cultural contexts, and the *intercultural literacy* which will allow them to interact effectively with conversation partners from differing cultural backgrounds. Forums suited to honing communicative and intercultural literacies include the wikis or Moodle VLEs which underpin many school 'e-twinning' (online partnership) programs, as well as worldwide discussion and networking sites like TakingITGlobal; and, at the other end of the spectrum, virtual worlds where students must navigate cultural mores as they customise and clothe their avatars, negotiate personal space and try to interpret body language!

Multiple languages and cultures are very much part of multiliteracies as conceived of by the New Literacy Studies movement and New London Group. It's worth remembering that, globally speaking, monolinguals are in the minority. While English remains the navigational lingua franca of the net, English speakers had declined to around 29 per cent of net users by March 2009[56] – meaning that monolingual Anglophones are excluded from more and more online interactions. It's salutary for students to get a feeling for the rich linguistic tapestry of our digital planet: pulling in RSS feeds in different languages, wading through the multilingual matrix of Twitter and Plurk, or participating in multicultural Facebook groups and Second Life meetings.

Most of all, though, students need access to learning opportunities which help them to relativise and reframe their own beliefs and perspectives. As one of my students put it towards the end of a semester's participation on a multicultural language teaching discussion board: 'Over the semester there was an overall shift from *must* to *might*'. In other words, by listening to and interacting with other teachers from other cultures with other kinds of teaching experiences, she'd learned to qualify her beliefs about the 'right' ways to teach, study and learn. On our small, overpopulated planet, we could all do with more of these kinds of lessons.

Technological literacy

Most students arrive at school, college or university with limited proficiency in the literacies we've been discussing, with the exception, for some, of remix literacy and the multiliteracy skills that underpin it. But the one area where many students regularly surpass their teachers is *technological literacy*; that is, the ability to use text and graphics software, web 2.0 applications and simple authoring tools, and the capacity to adapt to new tools as they become available. An inability to use such tools, with all of the flexibility and expressive possibilities they offer, is a serious limitation on twenty-first century literacy. There's little point in talking about information, participatory or intercultural literacy if you don't actually know how to comment on blogs, contribute to wikis or take part in virtual world forums; but if on the other hand you're familiar with blogs, wikis and virtual worlds, then it's essential to talk about information, participatory and intercultural literacy. To borrow two expressions from Gavin Dudeney, we need to distinguish between being 'tech-comfy' (which we might define as having the technological literacy to use a wide array of digital tools, especially for everyday social and entertainment purposes) and being 'tech-savvy' (having a grasp of technology's implications together with the range of digital literacies necessary to use key tools effectively for educational and professional purposes).[57] There's an opportunity here to combine (more tech-comfy) students' greater technological literacy with (more tech-savvy) teachers' greater expertise in information, participatory and intercultural literacies, to the benefit of both. And yet we should remember that some students' technological literacy is more limited or patchy than we might imagine: teachers are often surprised to discover that while a wiki, say, is no more remarkable to most students than a DVD player, many have never contributed to one and may even be unsure of how to do so. Teachers therefore have a responsibility to help these students, or help other students help them, acquire a basic command of technological literacy.

But there's also a growing need for a much deeper level of technological familiarity which we might call *code literacy*, involving the ability to read, write, critique and modify computer code. Without a measure of code literacy, even those who are able to make use of simple web applications will sometimes find themselves restricted to commercial or prepackaged options in place of customisable open source alternatives. After all, the code underpinning open source software is only really open, and hence generative, for those who can interpret and edit it. Marc Prensky calls this *programming literacy*, by which he means the ability 'to bend digital technology to one's needs, purposes, and will, just as in the present we bend words and images'. He envisions a future where '[l]iteracy will belong to those who can master not words, or even multimedia, but a variety of powerful, expressive human–machine interactions'.[58] This isn't about IT teachers and IT students. It's about IT as a core skill for all teachers and all students. It may well represent the biggest challenge yet for today's teachers and more than a few of today's students, but the literacy landscape of the future will be shaped mainly by those who can adapt – starting now.

Texting literacy

No discussion of contemporary literacies would be complete without a mention of the linguistic phenomenon which is the bane of conservative critics: 'txtspk', the language of rapid textual communication on mobile phones, or 'netspeak', the associated language of rapid textual communication on the net. It's been claimed that this language signals 'inordinate casualness, negligence, and lethargy';[59] that it is 'bleak, bald, sad shorthand';[60] and even that it is 'savaging our sentences' and 'raping our vocabulary'.[61] In fact, txtspk, which seems to exist in most languages, is a language practice well suited to rapid communication. At the same time it may also serve to demonstrate membership in the (younger) ranks of the technologically proficient and to display a touch of 'cool' vis-à-vis (older) parents and teachers, possibly with the added benefit of excluding the latter groups from eavesdropping on conversations. Unlike schoolyard language of the past, however, its use is far from restricted to the young.

Interestingly, research in both the US and UK suggests that most teens, unlike the Scottish 13-year-old we met at the start of the book, don't actually see texting as a kind of writing, even if elements of it sometimes slip into their academic work.[62] Nevertheless, they might well benefit from some instruction in *texting literacy* to raise their awareness of the still unstable features of txtspk, to help them contrast txtspk with more standard language, to give them practice in codeswitching between the two, and to assist them in differentiating the contexts appropriate to each. (And then if kids still choose to hand in essays about *baas &* ^^^^^ we can be sure it's not a linguistic issue!) In this way, rather than devaluing kids' pre-existing literacy skills, teachers can build on them while continuing to promote what, for now, remains standard language. And who knows whether a facility in txtspk may not be a more useful future skill for some of today's students than an ability to write traditional prose?

Something commonly missed by critics is the degree of creativity displayed in txtspk. It's part of a long 'European ludic linguistic tradition'[63] which makes clever use of visual and auditory elements, much like some contemporary advertising (Figure 3.3). At its best, it may be a sign of a very sophisticated command of language: the

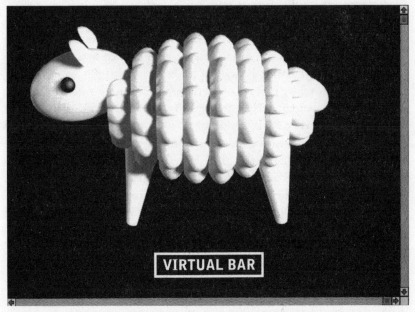

Figure 3.3. Language play. Image: Virtual Bar. © Guinness & Co.

ability to engage in linguistic games is, ironically, enhanced by a strong familiarity with the standard rules of print literacy – and a sense of when and how to break them.

Of course, language does evolve and some aspects of txtspk are already finding their way into offline (and standard) usage. On the other hand, its more extreme and idiosyncratic aspects may be very temporary, resulting from the limitations of keypads and keyboards, and may disappear with the spread of voice recognition and other new technologies. And yet maybe the kids have got it right, at least in part, and maybe the rest of us have something to learn from them. In fact, it would seem a shame not to use this window of opportunity to make a few changes to some of the needless historical complexities of English. In the spirit of Noah Webster, maybe we ought to seriously consider whether 'u' might be a sensible replacement for 'you', or 'i' for 'I', or whether apostrophes (a relatively recent addition to English) have outstayed their welcome except as stylistic features?

What could go wrong?

Post-industrial economies; web 2.0; social constructivist pedagogy; multiliteracies. It sounds like a perfect match. What could possibly go wrong? Quite a lot, actually.

Governments and institutions vs teachers

Ever since the rise of the European nation states, Western education systems have fulfilled a curiously contradictory double function: as a place for the reproduction of the social order, and as a space outside society in which to think differently. Periods of general liberalisation, as in the 60s, have been followed by periods of repression, as in more recent years. On the one hand, contemporary education has become increasingly subject to the neoliberal dictates of the market, with states seeing their role as providing a standardised workforce to compete in the global knowledge economy. On the other hand, in the context of the ongoing culture wars born out of the conservative backlash against 'the rise of feminism, multiculturalism and libertarian social attitudes in the 1960s and 1970s',[64] conservative governments (which may or may not be conservative in name) tend to view schools and colleges as a place to 'bring[ ] the nation to order'[65] in the face of an increasingly diverse society. The result is more and more centralised control through the imposition of national curricula, standardised testing, and performance and accountability measures. Of course, much depends on the detail of the curricula or tests, and sometimes standardisation is necessary, as we'll see. But none of these steps are especially likely to encourage social constructivist approaches, the exploration of web 2.0, the teaching of multiple literacies, or the fostering of the creative, flexible, collaborative skills needed by those who will run, rather than merely service, post-industrial economies.

Moreover, these steps are part of a long-running trend towards the deprofessionalisation of teachers, whose expert judgement and autonomy have gradually been eroded by governmental and bureaucratic controls.[66] At the same time, teachers are hampered by history in the form of vestiges of industrial-era schooling, ranging from 'rigid years, grades, terms and timetables'[67] to classroom walls which are impermeable to the outside world. And, to an equal extent, they are hampered by their own institutions' fearful attitudes towards technology. As noted in the 2008 Australia–New Zealand *Horizon Report*:

> Security concerns too often go too far. Both policies and firewalls are severely limiting access to—and hampering the utility of—the Internet, the use of digital materials, and many benefits of social networking. Adding to this, the mindset of central network planners and administrators is often at odds with the increasingly user-centric nature of Internet applications and tools, limiting innovation.[68]

One result of security concerns is growing repositories of transferable, sharable learning objects which effectively reduce teachers' creative choices to questions of sequencing. Another is the imposition of locked down, proprietary VLEs which replace brick-and-mortar classroom walls with virtual ones, limiting the power of both teachers and students to reconfigure learning spaces or use them imaginatively. Indeed, an important symbolic battle is taking shape around VLEs and PLEs. PLEs pack an impressive pedagogical punch but VLEs carry institutional clout. Hybrid solutions are possible in the form of open source VLEs like Moodle and Sakai, or purpose-built groups on Ning, which are more open to the wider web. But in many locations an all-or-nothing boxing match goes on between supporters of closed and open technology. The outcomes will tell us much about governments' and institutions' future pedagogical commitments.

In brief, social constructivist pedagogy, web 2.0 and multiple literacies are all about decentralising control and distributing authority. Post-industrial economies are all about abandoning one-size-fits-all approaches and diversifying connections. None are well served by governmental moves towards centralisation and standardisation, or institutional moves towards locked down, inflexible digital environments.

Literacy vs literacies

The conservative struggle to impose order on diversity takes many forms, but perhaps the greatest vehemence is found in literacy debates or, as one Australian commentator calls them, 'literacy wars'.[69] From observing centuries of language development, we know that in times of uncertainty or instability, grammar becomes a metaphorical battleground for the re-establishment of social order.[70] In our own time, this is compounded by the fact that, thanks to practices like txtspk, we're witnessing a genuinely rapid transformation of linguistic norms which usually evolve much more slowly. And these changes don't just relate to spelling, grammar or syntax, or even to style and formality, but to the use of the written word itself: after centuries of dominance in the modern period, written language is ceding ground to graphic elements (which are beginning to regain some of the prominence they held until the Middle Ages) and even audio elements. Not that it's a case of any one of these excluding the others: today's textuality, as we've seen, is relentlessly multimodal.

This leaves conservatives fighting a rearguard action under a 'back-to-basics' banner, and insisting, as one critic did in relation to the new national English curriculum being drafted in Australia, that the proposed inclusion of 'multi-modal texts' and 'graphic and other visual formats' in literature lessons is worrying because: 'Nothing should take away the primacy of the printed word'.[71] But the primacy of the printed word is already in the past. Socrates once protested the invention of writing, fearing its effect on memory and its deadening of discussion. Scrolls probably seemed infinitely more elegant to early readers than clumsy books. The Medieval Church must have shuddered at Gutenberg's printing press – its usefulness for printing indulgences notwithstanding – as it began to put the Word of God into the hands of laypeople. Today's conservatives, highly schooled in the modernist paradigm, fear what will now happen to the sustained, solitary reading of an elite canon of printed texts.

Such fears are never unfounded. With every change in literacy something is lost. But much is also gained. It's sometimes forgotten that books, like scrolls before them, and oral epics before those, were primarily a product of technological limitations. We read books the way we do because, for centuries, there was little alternative. Now there is. It's quite delusional to raise the technological limitations of past societies to principles worth defending at all costs. Yes, because we read them for so long, books affected our culture deeply. So too will digital documents, in different ways.

It's not the end of reading. Far from it. People are reading more than ever before – in a greater variety of formats. Nor, as we've noted, is it a case of abandoning print literacy or books, which will continue to play a vital role in fostering certain kinds of thinking and learning. Rather, it's about appreciating that the literacy landscape has dramatically diversified. Many of the new literacies are arguably more complex than monomodal, unidirectional, stable print literacy. And all of us – including the print literacy intelligentsia, many of whom are functionally illiterate in the emerging digital mediascape – will need to dramatically expand our skills to deal with these changes.

For the moment, liberals and conservatives are continuing to slog it out in the combat zone of contemporary literacies. The conservative notion that there's only one right way of doing things (and that it lies in the past) is a serious hindrance when it comes to educating students to navigate digital technologies and the broader post-industrial landscape. The future is less about *must*, and more about *might*. It requires a balance which many conservative commentators seem unwilling or unable to strike. They are entirely right to claim that traditional print literacy must not be neglected. But neither must digital literacies, which are so essential to the personal, social and professional futures of today's students, as well as to the political and economic futures of their societies.

Pedagogy vs pedagogies

Those who are critical of new literacies are equally likely to be critical of new pedagogies, preferring traditional transmission approaches linked to standardised content dictated by standardised curricula and assessed in standardised exams. All of which, naturally, lead to standardised students with standardised skills – which isn't ideal preparation for a post-industrial context.

But that doesn't mean there's no place for traditional ways of teaching and learning. Teachers need to appreciate the value of social constructivism and related approaches in preparing their students to participate, as employees and citizens, in digitally mediated societies. Yet they also need the confidence to make judicious pedagogical decisions, recognising when constructivism may not be the best choice and a more eclectic approach, drawing on older transmission or behaviourist methods, may be appropriate. That includes those times, particularly at foundational stages of learning, when there are factual or widely accepted bodies of knowledge to be transmitted and rehearsed, and where time is limited, so that it may be more suitable to use digital technology in pedagogically traditional ways (or not to use it at all). Yes, that's right, we're talking about standardised bodies of knowledge and standardised ways of testing. After all, as Jeff Jarvis notes, we need some safeguards against the 'citizen surgeon';[72] the same goes for the citizen engineer and the citizen architect. That's not to say newer pedagogies can't play a role in education in these areas, especially at higher levels, but without the basics in place students may derive limited value from autonomous explorations or peer collaborations, and they risk endangering themselves and others.

There is a place, Anna Sfard suggests, for both traditional acquisition and contemporary participation metaphors to be applied in education.[73] Even in the field of e-learning, notes Gary Motteram, course design should involve a balance between social constructivist and transmission approaches.[74] Apart from anything else, it's sheer hubris to imagine that humanity has only just learned how to teach and that teachers, methods and materials from the past (or for that matter, from other cultures with differing educational traditions) have nothing to offer us.

In this context, teacher trainers find themselves with a curious double imperative: firstly, persuading future teachers who've been schooled in traditional ways to become social constructivists; and secondly, persuading the same teachers that they don't have to be social constructivists *all* the time. For liberals, battling a tide of governmental, institutional and public pressure, it's important not to let constructivism become a dogma and to lose sight of the fact that teaching is, above all, contextual. It's entirely valid, depending upon level, subject and purpose, to combine newer with older approaches. For conservatives, battling to save the past from the present and future, it's time to realise there is no either/or choice to be made here. Pedagogy, like literacy, is plural. And balance is the key, though we need to place most emphasis on the engaging, collaborative pedagogies which will best prepare the majority of our students for the majority of roles they're likely to face in a post-industrial landscape.

Teachers vs teachers

Educators themselves are divided about the value of new technologies. For some, everything is different. The world is changing, says Gilly Salmon, putting 'pressure on educational institutions to respond to rapidly evolving business environments'. In open, cosmopolitan societies '[l]ong-living, long-working, independent learners will be mobile and pragmatic' and will be 'skilful in choosing from a vast electronic array of opportunities'.[75] Students have changed, says Marc Prensky, and have '*very different minds* from their parents and, in fact, *all* preceding generations [emphasis in original]'.[76] Indeed, he suggests that students are the only ones who really know how to embrace a changing world – implying that they're far ahead of their teachers not just technologically but pedagogically! In the words of Kip Leland, '[t]oday's kids are not ADD, they're EoE [Engage me or Enrage me]'.[77]

For others, little is – or should be – different. Naomi Baron states: 'It is very common to hear people say, Here's the Millennial or the digital generation, and we have to figure out how they learn. Poppycock. We get to mold how they learn'.[78] But it's Tara Brabazon who, with book titles like *Digital Hemlock: Internet Education and the Poisoning of Teaching* (2002) and *The University of Google: Education in the (Post) Information Age* (2007), has effectively become the face of academic protest against electronic technologies in education. Her 2008 statement, widely reported in the press, that Google and Wikipedia are the equivalent of 'white bread for the mind',[79] was a follow-up to earlier arguments:

> Education is not like browsing through a grocer, picking up the cheap, the delicious and the colourful. It is life-changing – and tough. By displacing this struggle, Internet learning has, so far, been a tragedy for education. It is a relaxed, ill-focused environment for the students who can least manage this pedagogic plasticity.[80]

Rejecting constructivism as 'the grammar of the techno-enthusiasts' which 'assumes that learners can build their own knowledge',[81] she insists, like Baron, on a strong role for educators.

Given the arguments we've heard over literacy and literacies, and pedagogy and pedagogies, it's unsurprising that teachers are divided in their views of technology and its role in the education of the younger generation. While these discussions sometimes stray into hyperbole, both of the opposing camps described here have useful insights and important warnings to offer. But perhaps the greatest danger is that, with the ongoing polarisation of the field, they will come to simply dismiss each other's ideas, engaging with each other less and less. Yet we need the insights and the warnings that both groups can provide as we seek a point of balance from which we can capitalise on the benefits of new technologies, new literacies and new pedagogies, while retaining the best of our educational heritage.

Teachers as learners

More than two decades ago, it was suggested that teachers are 'a bigger threat to computers than computers are to teachers'. What this means is that, with insufficient training, teachers are liable to adopt only 'the most trivial aspects of the new technology' as an add-on to current practices, without exploring technology's real affordances.[82] That is, of course, if they don't just reject it outright. This does neither teachers nor students any favours, with technology becoming ever more important thanks to the proliferation of digital tools. While many students are tech-comfy, few are tech-savvy – and some are neither, which leaves them to rely for guidance and motivation on staff who themselves may be floundering technologically. Teachers, then, need a certain level of technological competence. They need the confidence to bring technology out of the labs where it's cloistered away and make it part of the everyday curriculum. They need the self-assurance to venture beyond the restrictions of prepackaged software and explore open source software and free web services.

Teachers also need the pedagogical competence to work with digital technologies, understanding how contemporary pedagogies and literacies fit with web 2.0. That means they need the skills to deal with the heavy monitoring and mentoring demands of social constructivism, which are exacerbated by web 2.0's multiplication of communication channels and opportunities. They need the patience to explain the rationale for time-consuming collaborative activities to students who may be used to simpler and less demanding transmission or behaviourist approaches. Yet, as we've seen, they also need the experience to determine when new pedagogies, new literacies and new technologies are not most appropriate to their ends. And finally, they need the confidence to combine their pedagogical expertise with their students' technical expertise, which may sometimes outstrip their own, as they build twenty-first century teaching and learning partnerships in their classes.

"Class, I've got a lot of material to cover, so to save time I won't be using vowels today. Nw lts bgn, pls pn t pg 122."

Figure 3.4. Teaching in an age of digital literacies. Cartoon © Randy Glasbergen, 1997, <www.glasbergen.com>.

But it's about more than pedagogical competence, too. Teachers have to appreciate the limitations of new technologies. Education isn't always well served by the association of the net with entertainment – as captured in the net 'surfing' metaphor[83] – or student expectations of convenience and flexibility. The speed of information transfer and communication can erode the space for reflection, and it's easy to engage in only a superficial, fragmentary way with online content. Surveillance and censorship are becoming pressing issues as digital technology blurs the boundaries between the private and the public. Collective intelligence, for all its advantages, may sometimes fail us when it comes to diversity or tolerance. And technology comes with a price, paid by our minds, our bodies and our planet. Given such issues, it's imperative that teacher training covers far more than technology and pedagogy. Educators need a clear sense of the social, sociopolitical and ecological embeddedness of technology (which we'll explore in the following chapters) in order to incorporate it effectively into their teaching.

The need for such a wide swathe of competencies places considerable demands on educational trainers and trainees, not to mention on funding bodies. Traditionally, governments and educational institutions have understood the need to spend money on hardware and software, even if they've subsequently tried to limit how innovatively it's used through standardisation or security measures. However, they've rarely acknowledged the need to spend similar amounts of money on the 'wetware' – the human competence – essential to making the most of technology. A cynic might see the current lack of high-level training for teachers in many parts of the world as ideally suited to keeping the lid on real pedagogical innovation around new technologies. Yet there's pressure to change, and there are promises of change, in this area. A 2007 report on ICTs prepared for the Australian Department of Education, Science and Training emphasised the importance of a massively increased focus on teacher training and professional development, including the need:

> to equip educators with an available, state-of-the-art underpinning theoretical framework so that they are better placed to guide teaching and learning efforts, to convert hunches and intuition into demonstrable student gains and, genuinely, to innovate.[84]

It can only be hoped that the current Australian Government's Digital Education Revolution, like similar initiatives elsewhere, delivers on the human aspects of its promises. There's no substitute for well-trained educators who, through careful planning and intensive engagement with technological, pedagogical and broader issues, can maximise the educational relevance of digital technologies.

Living in educational beta

It's difficult to imagine educators completely jettisoning standard language. Education, after all, has to balance the old and the new. But right now, there's a lot that's new, much of it driven by or derived from digital technologies. Digital technologies underpin the creative networking of post-industrial economies. Digital technologies lend themselves to constructivist, collaborative pedagogies. Digital technologies demand cooperative, tentative literacies. And, despite the standardisation plans of governments, the security restrictions of educational institutions, the back-to-basics campaigns of conservative critics, the anti-digital campaigns of conservative educators, and the underfunding of teacher training, there's real educational potential in the overlap between digital, post-industrial, social constructivist and multiple literacies paradigms. It's just as well. It's been said that much of contemporary education is about preparing students for jobs that don't yet exist.[85] We're living not just in perpetual technological beta, but in perpetual educational and professional beta as well. But while we can't imagine, much less guarantee, what the jobs of the future will be, we can be fairly sure that they will occur in post-industrial contexts, will involve digital technologies, and will require multiple literacies. And, notwithstanding the crucial need for balance, we can be fairly sure that social constructivism and related pedagogies provide good preparation for these conditions, helping students develop relevant skillsets – and open mindsets.

But education is more than job preparation. Those who can't express themselves effectively online, whether that involves older skills derived from the print literacy paradigm or the cluster of newer skills which make up digital literacies, are doomed to silence in digital culture. They'll find themselves on the wrong side of a digital divide which, ultimately, is as much a literacy as an economic issue.[86] That's why education must also prepare students for a social future where they have the technological and personal literacies to build their own digital identities and author their own individual narratives. It must prepare them for a sociopolitical future where they have the participatory and remix literacies to intervene in societal narratives. It must prepare them for a global future where they have the cultural and intercultural literacies to contribute to world narratives. The future of our individual liberties, our democratic political systems and our planet demands it.

4

Many selves

A social lens

'Online mob trashes birthday party' (*The Observer*, 16 March 2008). 'Kids try to derail train for internet glory' (*The Australian*, 26 September 2008). 'UK children at greater risk from online predators as they spend more time indoors' (*The Daily Telegraph*, 27 September 2008). 'Teen "sexting" craze leading to child porn arrests in US' (*The Times*, 14 January 2009). 'Greatest internet threat to teens may be teens themselves' (*Los Angeles Times*, 26 January 2009).

The media, with pollsters, parents and politicians in tow, speculate endlessly about the so-called 'net generation', 'net gen', 'digital natives', 'millennials', 'generation Y' or 'gen Y', worrying alternately that they are a serious danger (to themselves and others) or seriously endangered (by themselves and others). News headlines are a litany of anguish and incomprehension over a younger generation that seems so different from preceding generations. And that's before we get into tabloid territory... But if parents and teachers are to offer young people some guidance and direction, we need a more balanced understanding of the net generation. We need to figure out how they're building their identities and socialising online. We need to figure out where the real dangers lie and where they don't. We need to figure out what's really changed and what really hasn't. And we need to figure out what all this means for young people's evolving life stories.

Would the real net generation please stand up?

Firstly, though, we need to figure out what the net generation – defined by Don Tapscott as those born between 1977 and 1997 – actually is.[1] We're told it's 'hardly worth mentioning anymore' that today's students 'are very computer-savvy'.[2] We're told it's 'the first time in human history when children are authorities on something really important'.[3] This is partly because young people haven't been limited by a pre-digital mindset about what can be done with computers. It's also partly because they've had the time to play with the technology, which is often the best way to discover how it works. Their resulting level of technological literacy is something many older people find unsettling.

And yet simple terms like 'net generation' may blind us to a more complex reality. A swathe of studies has shown that factors like geographic location (including the rural/urban divide), socioeconomic status, education, race, language and gender also have a dramatic impact on net use.[4] What's more, age, the major factor relied on in definitions of the net generation, turns out to be a less accurate predictor than is usually assumed. There are plenty of people aged 30-plus who are far more literate in the new medium than those born from '77 to '97. In fact, the whole concept is a somewhat simplistic projection by bemused (and mostly unwired) older people onto unsuspecting youngsters who, even if they use digital technologies extensively, would never define themselves as a 'net generation' any more than their elders would have called themselves a 'TV generation' or a 'radio generation'.[5]

So, although it's true that lots of young people are technologically very accomplished, particularly if they're well educated and live in affluent, urban, Western or Westernised communities, the picture is more complicated than catch-all terms like 'net generation' or 'digital natives' imply. Many young people don't write in netspeak, keep blogs or regularly upload videos to YouTube. Many state that they prefer only a moderate use of technology in education.[6] Many lack key digital literacies. In brief, 'young' ≠ 'tech-comfy' ≠ 'tech-savvy', though there's obviously some overlap. The reality is that most of today's students would benefit from guidance on how to make the best use of – and avoid the worst dangers of – electronic tools in all areas of their lives: not just academically and professionally, but personally and socially as well.

Writing your/self into being
Relating (to) the self

The Swedish nurse who posted Facebook pictures taken while she was assisting with brain surgery,[7] and the British juror who used Facebook to ask friends whether they thought defendants in a trial were guilty,[8] are early casualties in a massive, unplanned social experiment, where the rules for self-presentation and socialisation are evolving minute by minute. You can write yourself into being on the net.[9] Digital technologies, which allow – and increasingly, require – you to compose, edit and revise your own story, effectively extend the growing individualisation of society that's been underway since at least the late 60s.[10] It might be argued that sometimes it's less about writing (linear) stories and more about creating (spatial) displays of various facets of the self,[11] but the key point – that you have the ability to author your own story or craft your own display – remains the same. Still, digital literacy is tricky. It's easy to write your narrative badly or organise your display clumsily and find yourself misunderstood or ostracised…and out of a relationship or a job.

Exploring your identity online, on the simplest level, can mean delving into the spectrum of perspectives and lifestyles to which the net gives you access. At some point, though, you may well feel compelled to take a more active role, trying out different aspects of your personality in public forums like social networking sites or blogs. As Sarah Boxer found in her exploration of the blogosphere:

> Some [bloggers] use [the internet] as a writing prod. Some use it as a trash can. Some use it like a diary. Some use it like a pulpit. Some use it like a drawing pad. Some use it like a padded room. Some use it to reach out. Some use it to reach in. Some use it to get mad. Some use it to get even.[12]

As you experience reactions to your musings, rants or confessions, you can begin to construct a narrative that reflects a self, or selves, that represent who you are or want to be. Most of us already do this every day in our offline lives. The net just gives us more diverse options, contexts and audiences. That's very important for young people, who are at a stage of life when it's normal to explore and experiment with self-presentation, but who don't always have a lot of offline opportunities for addressing a wider public.[13] It's especially important for those who feel they need the cover of partial or complete anonymity to present aspects of themselves they'd otherwise hide. The net, as Lawrence Lessig has said, 'enables lives that were previously impossible, or inconvenient, or uncommon'.[14] Part of the reason is that online experiences translate back into offline ones.

Sure, there are some people who use the net as an escape route and whose storytelling freedom exists only online. But research indicates that for most people, most of the time, online identities are closely related to offline identities.[15] We also know that youth in particular use the net to come to terms with aspects of their lives they're struggling with, ranging from depression and fear to alternative sexualities. This gives them the chance of 'reconfiguring actual, possible, and ideal selves in various arrangements', reworking them in light of feedback and, especially in response to positive feedback, integrating their online self-presentations with their offline selves.[16] But in a sense the net's freedom to keep reimagining and remodelling ourselves makes eternal teenagers – or Foucault's artworks-in-progress – of all of us.

In the 90s, the net was sometimes portrayed as an out-of-control identity workshop where people in early chatrooms and virtual environments randomly swapped genders, races and sexualities, pushing their own and each other's boundaries in the process. While some such experimentation certainly did and does occur, it's turned out to be far less widespread than was once assumed.[17] That may be just as well: it's naive to suggest that role-playing other genders or races gives you more than a superficial glimpse of alternative realities. It's utopian to think that such 'identity tourism' is appealing to many people outside an educated,

Figure 4.1. Building an online identity? Cartoon © Dave Walker, 2006, <www.cartoonchurch.com>.

leisured Western elite. Notwithstanding the freedoms the net offers to the incapacitated or disabled,[18] it's foolish to imagine you can really escape your own body online and simply slough off your gender, race and sexuality. In fact, it's more than foolish: as we'll see in Chapter 6, it's highly dangerous to try to escape into a purely mental realm and dismiss your own body or the larger environment which sustains it.

There are other dangers, too. Will a protracted focus on building identity and narrative on – literally and metaphorically – 'egocentric' social networking sites[19] lead to empty digital narcissism and a whole generation of self-proclaimed micro-celebrities? Will kids become addicted to social networking or gaming sites, resigning themselves to the offline status quo as long as they have online autonomy? Do the net's endless promises to make everyone more attractive, more desirable and more virile exacerbate the insecurities of the young and the vulnerable? What if teens choose the wrong contexts in which to reveal sensitive personal information? And what if individuals egg each other on to build not the 'wisdom of the crowd' but the 'brutality of the mob', venting their spite on those who are different or defenceless, or who are just in the wrong place at the wrong time? The digital world can be as cruel and unforgiving as the analogue one and, as we'll see, has a much longer memory...

Educational intervention in this area is long overdue. Teachers can seek, firstly, to help students expand their narrative options as they refine their control over a variety of literacies, which will give them the tools to shape their own stories and provide the metacommentary on their own lives. Secondly, teachers have a duty to offer students some guidance on the yawning pitfalls of online life, ranging from the false promises of identity tourism to the false promises of spam, and from the trap of too readily exposing your innermost thoughts to the trap of getting caught up in the cybermob. To deny students access to digital literacies and digital warnings in the name of an outdated, pre-digital model of education is nothing short of irresponsible.

Relating to others

Contrary to common perceptions, studies show that socialising online correlates highly with socialising offline. Social networking, blogging and even gaming can all be good for your social life.[20] At the same time, the net is becoming a natural complement to the most important moments of our offline social lives: from the live feeds which allow once-absent friends to participate in distant weddings, to distributed funerals like that of Randy Pausch in 2008, where mourning spread across an interlinked network of blogs and tweets.[21]

If individuals can increasingly write their own stories on the net, they can also increasingly choose the social contexts in which these stories unfold and which, in turn, feed back into their stories. Sociologists see the net as supporting a larger pattern of networked individualism, leading to the development of 'networks of sociability based on choice and affinity' rather than geography or social tradition.[22] Nevertheless, the majority of the people we interact with online are the same ones we interact with offline. Young or old, people mostly use digital technologies to overcome factors like distance (too much) and time (too little) in order to maintain and extend pre-existing relationships.[23] The difference is more choice over *which* relationships to maintain and extend.

Some critics worry that digital relationships aren't real because you can just switch off your computer (or mobile) any time you want.[24] But do that a couple of times and you'll soon find yourself as isolated from online networks as you would from offline ones if you walked out of the room every time you didn't like what someone said. Other critics worry that we 'confuse data transfer with human communication' online,[25] but they fail to appreciate that it's not about settling for less but about communicating differently. The apparent inanities exchanged on mobile phones are examples of what linguists call 'phatic communication', whose purpose is social rather than informational. In other words, it's not about conveying specific content but about saying: I'm here, I'm OK, I'm thinking of you.[26] In the same way, the endless, frequently

"WELL, YES, WE COULD READ YOUR BLOG.... OR YOU COULD JUST TELL US ABOUT YOUR SCHOOL DAY."

Figure 4.2. The social consequences of blogging? Cartoon: Jim Borgman © Cincinnati Enquirer. Reprinted with permission of Universal Press Syndicate. All rights reserved.

banal status updates on social networking and microblogging services are about maintaining 'ambient intimacy' with friends and acquaintances; that is, sustaining a kind of 'social peripheral vision' that keeps you in touch with others' lives.[27] As we've seen before, something is always lost when a mode of communication changes, but something is also gained. Despite frequently expressed concerns about the consequences of diminishing face-to-face interaction, surveys consistently find that net and mobile technologies help users to communicate *more* and *better* than previously with family and friends.[28]

Digital interaction is becoming especially important for kids as adults continue to restrict their access to the places they used to hang out: malls, parks, local streets. In today's risk-averse culture, more and more nervous parents are keeping their kids indoors despite their normal, developmental need to spend time with their peers and take risks in a social context.[29] In other words, much of what kids are doing online is what kids have always done. They're just forced to do it digitally. And it's absolutely essential to their socialisation into wider online and offline society.

But there are differences, too, between online and offline contact. Not only do digital social networks reinforce a relatively small number of strong bonds to family and friends through regular interaction, they also help to preserve, or even create, a much larger number of so-called 'weak ties'.[30] Many of the 'friends' you collect on social networking sites are not friends in a traditional sense. Some are old classmates, former colleagues and friends of friends met at parties; in short, acquaintances who might normally drift away as your life paths diverge. Others may be contacts you've made online through communities of interest or professional forums; that is, people you've never met face-to-face. These ties, once formed, can be maintained, built on and strengthened. Weak ties have important benefits. On the one hand, they're beginning to fulfil some of the needs traditionally fulfilled by local communities.[31] On the other, it's probable that having a large digital network of weak ties – which can be activated as necessary in the future to help with, say, finding jobs – may become an important component of the 'social capital' which kids build up early in life and which will contribute to their professional success as adults.[32] (Indeed, weak ties are the main driver of LinkedIn, the very successful professional social networking site.[33]) Treating friendship as philately, as one critic sees it,[34] may thus turn out to have long-term advantages. It's yet another reason educators must insist that kids from less advantaged backgrounds, who may not have home computer access, are not shut out of networking sites in schools and libraries.

Of course, strong relationships can also come into being online. Cyberspace offers 'a unique environment for people to experience and learn about relationships and sexuality', especially for those who are lonely or shy.[35] And more and more relationships – friendly, romantic and/ or sexual – are crossing the highly permeable online/offline border in both directions. A key fear for many adults is the digitalisation of youth sexual exploration. Certainly, digital technologies are playing a growing role in young people's sex lives. In 2008, a large-scale survey of 13 to 26-year-olds in the US found that 27 per cent overall (and 33 per cent of those in their twenties) had sent or posted nude or semi-nude photos or videos of themselves, while 49 per cent (and 59 per cent of those in their twenties) had sent or posted sexually suggestive messages.[36] When it involves mobile phones, this is referred to as 'sexting'. If only 5 per cent of people engage in sexting, it's a minority pursuit. When 50 per cent or more do so, it becomes the new normal. For the younger generation, the internet and digital technologies are part of their sexual future as much as they're part of their social and professional futures.

For the population at large, the net has two main effects on sexuality. Firstly, it's a source of detailed information. Although there's the ever-present danger of misinformation, there's also the chance for individuals to explore health or psychological issues in an unpressured environment and to communicate confidentially with others facing similar issues.[37] Secondly, the net facilitates sexual contact and experimentation, once again furthering the liberalising ethos of the 60s. In the long run, its greatest benefits will likely be for sexual minorities. Given the diversity of human sexuality, the net allows more people than ever before to connect with others who can offer them fulfilment.

But there's also a lot that can go wrong, even if much of it is simply a digital twist on the offline world. Potential hazards extend from the development of intimacy issues to the loss of privacy and the threat of cyberstalking. Young people, moreover, are at a vulnerable stage of development. There are concerns over the psychological effects of early exposure to online porn: it has been claimed, for example, that this may lead to skewed views of 'normal' sexual behaviour[38] (though normality in this area is surely a matter of perspective). There are concerns, too, over peer pressure to engage in sexting and the possible result, namely the uncontrolled and uncontrollable circulation of kids' own sexual images. Other issues range from the spread of child porn – including through sexting, which in the US has already led to the bizarre situation of children being prosecuted as child pornographers[39] – to the risk of inappropriate liaisons. We'll look at these dangers in more detail shortly.

Surely, though, open discussion and guidance at an early age would be much more productive than meting out hefty punishments to kids who get caught sexting, while effectively refusing to engage young people in talking about practices which, for them, are rapidly becoming part of everyday life.

There are also other, quite different risks associated with a social life lived largely online. The net is an amazingly diverse place. Yet most people miss out on most of the diversity most of the time. Thanks to personalised search results, filtered RSS feeds and our growing attachment to social networks, it's easy to spend lots of time in online 'echo chambers' where you only encounter views you already agree with. Some 91 per cent of political blogs have been found to link exclusively to politically similar sites; MySpace users have been found to interact most often with others who share their ethnicity, religion, age, country, marital status and sexual orientation.[40] The more one-sided perspectives we encounter, and the more encouragement our pre-existing views receive, the greater the danger that social divisions will be deepened and prejudices reinforced. We could, as Nick Carr writes, 'click our way to a fractured society'.[41] Then again, how different is this from our offline lives? As David Weinberger puts it:

> How much time in the day do you spend talking rationally and calmly about matters of state with people with whom you disagree? [...] Have you ever actually sat down for a long, respectful conversation with a neo-Nazi or an out-of-the-closet racist, a conversation in which you're open to having your ideas changed?

> Me neither.[42]

Yet it's probably harder to avoid noticing different people, lifestyles and attitudes in the offline world (at least for those of us who live surrounded by an urban jumble of races, religions and socioeconomic classes) even if we don't really engage with difference offline any more than we do online. The main point is not to fall into the common trap of assuming that potential access to diversity on the internet will translate into actual access, or that it will promote tolerance and understanding. There's a real need here for educational intervention, with skilful teachers framing and scaffolding students' encounters with difference.

A more immediate and perhaps somewhat contrary danger has been referred to by danah boyd as 'context collisions' or 'collapsed contexts'. Essentially, the more people you're connected to, the harder it is to navigate the norms and expectations of the different audiences you're addressing in a single forum like Facebook or MySpace.[43] This is an issue for many young people. It's clearly also an issue for many older people, like the Swedish nurse and the British juror we met earlier. Yet it's even more complex than the notion of different audiences might at first suggest. In fact, it's about different selves.

A unitary self

In 2006, Hong Kong's 'Bus Uncle' achieved unexpected fame when a bus passenger secretly recorded him verbally abusing another passenger who'd asked him to talk more quietly on his mobile phone. The video was later posted on the net, where it's still available in multiple versions on YouTube, including one remixed to a soundtrack by Canto popstar Sammi Cheng. The Bus Uncle's story had a less than happy ending. He was eventually tracked down and beaten up at the restaurant where he worked: you can watch the news reports of that, too, on YouTube.[44] This story raises a number of uncomfortable questions about privacy, surveillance and the self.

We're all in the process of creating long, winding digital 'data trails', mostly in less dramatic fashion than the Bus Uncle – but usually with much more personal input. And like him, we may soon find ourselves unable to escape their effects in both our online and offline lives. After all, what happens to your old blog postings, your old status updates and your old digital pics when you have no more use for them? Think they'll eventually disappear into the ether? Think again. Three things have changed. Firstly, data storage has become cheap and effectively limitless. Secondly, digital data is easily searchable, with Google taking seconds to deliver information that might once have required an analogue lifetime to uncover...if the relevant data had even been recorded or stored in the first place. Thirdly, more and more digital data is being generated about all of us, some of it by ourselves (in our blog postings or shared videos), some by friends (with every comment they append to our status updates or photos), some by friends of friends (been tagged in any party snaps recently?), and some by strangers (like fellow bus passengers!). And that's without mentioning the information recorded by companies and governments, which we'll come back to in the next chapter.

We all choose to display different selves – or aspects of ourselves – for different purposes in different contexts. That's not to say these selves are entirely discontinuous, as suggested in some more radical readings of postmodernism, but they're certainly tailored to specific contexts and don't necessarily translate well into other contexts. So, here's the irony. On the one hand, digital technologies offer us unprecedented freedom to experiment with different facets of our identities and rework our life stories. On the other hand, digital technologies are relentlessly building data trails which preserve records of our every statement and action and may, ultimately, force each of us to adopt a more unitary identity than was ever the case in the analogue world.[45] Perhaps the context collisions of Facebook are just a mild foretaste of a world of pervasive digital records. Will kids one day be held to ransom for their youthful mistakes? Will adults be linked forever to their indiscreet comments or actions? Will we all end up paying a high price for our online experimentation – or our offline experimentation that's recorded online, as more and more of it will be?[46]

There are those who have a vested interest in locking individuals into unitary identities. Companies and governments, as we'll see later, head up the list. Employers also understandably insist on unitary identities in the workplace, with many keeping track of employees' emails and web surfing. However, recent cases of actual and threatened sackings, disciplinary proceedings, and promotions denied on the basis of social networking profiles unconnected to workplace roles show that employers are using digital technologies to extend demands for unitary identities into employees' non-working lives.[47] Job applicants are regularly Googled and checked out on Facebook, as are applicants at some US colleges. Parents, too, are busily combing MySpace, Facebook and mobile phone records in an effort to sew together the different pieces of their kids' multifaceted digital personas. Adults' enthusiasm for keeping tabs on each other manifests itself in a variety of ways, ranging from Western vengeance blogs, whose aim is to prevent ex-lovers or ex-friends ever escaping past actions, to China's human flesh search engines, made up of net users who digitally track and identify individuals they believe to have transgressed moral or social codes, with the aim of dispensing retribution...online and offline.[48]

Back in 1999, Scott McNealy, Chairman of Sun Microsystems, famously stated: 'You have zero privacy anyway. Get over it'.[49] There are two distinct conclusions we could draw from this. The first, typically drawn by the older generation, is exemplified by Barack Obama's minute vetting of assistants' email, blogging and social networking histories. It's about playing it safe and avoiding controversial comments or associations, effectively treating the web as a 'never-ending global job interview'.[50] The second conclusion, typically drawn by the younger generation, is that you should be completely open on the basis that, if everyone has a past that's public, no one can hold anything over you. Is this an ingenious strategy perfectly in tune with the times – or the height of naivety?

There are some reasons to think it might be ingenious. It's only a matter of time before those doing the admitting, employing and parenting will have their own messy digital dossiers. Writers for publications from *The Observer* to *The Economist* have toyed with the idea that 'mutually assured humiliation' might teach us all a lesson about tolerance.[51] And a few savvy kids like the gay American videoblogger Chris Crocker (of 'Leave Britney alone!' fame) have managed to turn themselves into media celebrities on the back of all the digital attention, absorbing and magnifying the lesson of the wider culture that there's no such thing as bad publicity. But there are also some reasons to think this strategy might be naive. Once the information is out there, it's too late to change your mind: you can't get it back. It'll also be a while before the digital immigrants hand over the reins of colleges, companies and governments. And companies and governments in particular are becoming much, much more interested in the unitary identities of their customers and citizens.

Enter education. In the murky area of digital identity, many kids and more than a few adults, including some teachers, are desperately in need of guidance. We have to start, then, with teacher training. And we have to start with facts. Research indicates that many young people, again like much of the broader population, are unaware of the nature and extent of the data trails they're generating.[52] People need to understand where all this data is coming from: what they generate themselves, what friends, acquaintances and even strangers generate, as well as what they give away to websites and bureaucracies. After that, we get into speculative territory where our goal must be to ensure that everyone does, in fact, begin to speculate: thinking through the possible consequences of their pics and postings for college admission or jobs, for future friendships and relationships, and for other aspects of their lives. Sexting is, potentially at least, forever. Kids have got to know that. A command of digital literacies means not only having the tools to craft an online persona, but having an understanding that at least some of what you say and do may matter in the long term. The shadow side of a planned e-portfolio as a CV is an unplanned data trail as a CV.

No one wants to end up like the Bus Uncle. Naturally, the man has a name, but he's been reduced to this public moniker. Naturally, he has other selves but he's found himself publicly reduced to a single self. Despite later interviews and media coverage, his ability to tell his own story, in analogue or digitally, is now seriously impaired. He is, first and last, the Bus Uncle, and always will be. It's an extreme case, for sure, and his level of control was limited except in the original incident. However, there's still much we can learn from this case and others like it.

Digital data doesn't go away. It's pervasive, searchable and can attach itself permanently to an individual, with consequences for life offline as well as online. The net can be a great place to experiment with and build an identity or identities, but carelessly or inadvertently generated data trails can turn it into an identity prison.

Dangerous or endangered?

We've seen that for youth and others, digital technologies offer empowering story writing tools. There are pitfalls, too, ranging from the narcissism of those on one side of the digital divide to the exclusion of those on the other. And it seems we're all in danger of becoming entangled in our own data trails which may, after all, force us into unitary identities not entirely of our own choosing. But from the point of view of the media and the general public, these matters pale into insignificance compared with today's burning issue: young people's online safety.

Cybersafety

It's an old chestnut. We encounter it every time a new communications technology arrives on the scene and threatens to remove individuals from familial and social protection – or, depending on your point of view, to liberate them from familial and social control. The following two comments, made exactly a century apart, show how little has changed:

> The doors may be barred and a rejected suitor kept out, but how is the telephone to be guarded? (1905)

> You think your kid is safe because they are in your house in their own bedroom. Who can hurt them when you are guarding the front door? But [the internet] is a bigger opening than the front door. (2005)[53]

The term 'moral panic', used by Stanley Cohen to capture the fearful reaction to the behaviour of mods and rockers in 1960s Britain, is a good way of describing media-driven frenzies like the one we're currently witnessing around kids and the internet. In such cases, there's typically a 'dialectic of youth-in-trouble and troubling-youth', as Charles Acland puts it.[54] In other words, as Kate Crawford and Gerard Goggin explain, '[y]outh culture becomes the site of contest between the replication of the social order (conformism) and the resistance or rejection of pre-existing norms'.[55]

Of course, it's essential not to downplay the dangers for kids using digital technologies. Internet-related rapes, suicides and even murders are not unknown. We need to take kids' safety very seriously. What we don't need, though, is ill-informed media hype or political spin fuelling a moral panic and in the process obscuring what's actually happening online – thereby preventing us from intervening appropriately. The real risks for kids fall into three main categories, but none is what it seems at first glance.

The first risk, which was the subject of the first wave of public hysteria around kids and the net in the mid-1990s, is exposure to *cyberporn* or other inappropriate materials (for example, websites promoting hate speech or self-harm). However, an extensive review of recent research, carried out by the Internet Safety Technical Task Force for the US State Attorneys General and published at the end of 2008, has concluded that younger children, who are more often distressed by such material, are most likely to encounter it through offline sources, including magazines, TV and the movies. And while unwanted exposure certainly can and does occur on the net, it's also clear that many kids, especially male adolescents, purposely seek it out.[56] What's more, as we've seen, some kids are naively creating child porn themselves through sexting or posting images online.

The second risk, and the source of most current media hysteria, is *cyberpredation*. Yet statistics show a steady overall decline in sexual offences against children,[57] while the number of online stranger offenders is also falling.[58] The result is that the frequently invoked bogeyman of the online paedophile actually 'distract[s] us from more statistically significant molesters'[59] – family members and acquaintances, who are responsible for some 95 per cent of reported sexual assaults on children.[60] In other words, kids are in far more danger in their living rooms and bedrooms when they're *not* online than when they are. But the picture is even more complex than this: as we've seen, older youth are beginning to explore their own emerging sexuality online just as they do offline. We shouldn't be surprised to learn that 90 to 94 per cent of solicitations of minors where the approximate age of the sexual solicitor is known come from other minors or young adults. What's more, in cases which do involve adults – who are mostly young adults – it's often teens who initiate the sexual contact.[61]

Statistics show that the third risk, which is the subject of growing attention in the press, is by far the most significant: *cyberbullying*, which, depending on how bullying is defined, has been found to affect between 4 per cent and 46 per cent of youth,[62] though one recent study puts it as high as 72 per cent.[63] It's nearly always a case of peer bullying, meaning that the net generation is far more of a danger to itself than adult bullies (or adult predators) are. And there's often overlap between cyberbullies and bullying victims,[64] meaning that it's a self-perpetuating cycle. What makes cyberbullying potentially more devastating than offline bullying is its reach (with changing room photos or happy slapping videos being circulated widely at the click of mouse), its permanency (since, as we know, it's almost impossible to completely erase anything once it's posted on the net), and in extreme cases its potential to spiral into geographically dispersed mob bullying (as experienced by some unfortunate participants, both young and old, in recent reality TV shows). Yet, while this is real cause for concern, research suggests cyberbullying is less common than offline bullying.[65] There's certainly a lot of continuity between online and offline bullying: cyberspace, rather than being a qualitatively different environment, largely 'extends the school grounds'.[66]

Making the net safer

To date, adults' confused and reactionary responses, mostly involving legal or technical interventions, have done little to help young people. At one extreme, with children being prosecuted as child pornographers, it's arguable that they've actually harmed them. But by far the most common solution proposed to the problems of pornographers, predators and bullies is to filter the net. As a stand-alone measure, this won't work – and is harmful in its own way. Used differentially, PC-level filtering, which can be customised by parents or teachers to suit varying contexts, can play a part in a holistic net safety strategy for youth. Proponents of filtering, however, often push for its implementation at internet service provider (ISP) level, which usually entails a nationwide, one-size-fits-all system (even if it permits a limited number of differing access levels). Such filtering – as is currently being proposed, for example, by the Rudd Government in Australia (see Chapter 5 for details) – is a simplistic response to a complex, multifaceted situation.

Here's why. Most filters focus primarily on web content. They can filter out some porn websites, but they're generally not very effective at screening interactive channels like IM or chat, or indeed the whole range of peer-to-peer (p2p) traffic which has been estimated to make up between 60 and 72 per cent of global internet traffic.[67] That means they have little to contribute to problems like cyberbullying or cyberpredation, which mainly occur through IM or chat. Nor are they very useful when it comes to screening more extreme sexual material like adult-created child porn, which is usually not found on the open web, but is traded in encrypted form through p2p networks. What's more, filters are easy to circumvent through proxies, virtual private networks (VPNs) or onion routing software like Tor. In 2007, a 16-year-old Australian schoolboy, Tom Wood, took just over 30 minutes to crack the Howard Government's NetAlert filter, and 40 minutes to crack an upgraded version.[68] Ironically, under a home or school filtering system, technically minded teens may be able to access explicit material more easily than their parents or teachers. Filters also typically underblock, that is, fail to block access to a certain percentage of banned material. In short, net filters lead to an easy, but fundamentally flawed, illusion of safety.

Filters don't only underblock, they also overblock; that is, they restrict access to sites they shouldn't. Naturally, any content censorship which focuses on sexual material will impact most severely on minorities whose sexual orientations and practices are part of their self-definition. For example, a whole swathe of gay, lesbian, bisexual and transgender websites – whether with a community, dating or self-help focus, and whether accessed by youth, adults, or both – may be caught in filters.[69] And depending on the extent of the filtering, and the extent to which adults can opt out of it, there is a potentially serious impact on freedom of speech. '[P]erhaps', as one US judge wrote recently, 'we do the minors of this country harm if First Amendment protections, which they will with age inherit fully, are chipped away in the name of their protection'.[70] The same principle surely applies in all democracies, whether or not they have explicit constitutional free speech protections.

In Australia, where the Howard Government's NetAlert program made optional PC-level filters freely available to parents, it was estimated that only about 29,000 (less than 2 per cent of the government's target) were actually used on an ongoing basis,[71] suggesting that parents overwhelmingly reject government interference in this area. When ISP-level child-friendly filters are imposed by government, it disempowers parents, removing their ability to customise filters and to decide when and how to begin teaching their children to deal with online dangers. It also disempowers teachers, whose role it is to help parents educate young people to use the net in productive ways, ensuring that the digital literacies they acquire in school include a component of digital safety. And it disempowers young people themselves, making them beholden to an overprotective state, instead of allowing their parents and teachers to guide them on the path to becoming independent citizens who, in time, can reach their own decisions about how to safely navigate the virtual universe.

Technology, in the form of optional filters used under supervision, can play a role in cybersafety. At the other end of the spectrum, law enforcement is essential in the most serious cases. But instead of relying too heavily on technological or legal strategies, we have to confront social issues with social – and educational – strategies. This isn't new: cyberporn is a kind of porn; cyberpredation is a kind of predation; and cyberbullying is a kind of bullying. The net gives each of these new inflections, but the underlying problems are the same ones parents and teachers have always had to deal with. We make a fundamental mistake if we think kids are in danger just because of the net. They're not.

Moreover, research clearly shows that the young people who are at most risk online are the same ones who are at most risk offline. In other words, the greatest online dangers are faced by the kids with the most troubled backgrounds, including those who come from conflict-ridden home environments, have poor relationships with their parents, or have experienced physical and/or sexual abuse.[72] In some ways, oddly, the net is a boon to anyone who wants to help kids: problematic behaviours and interactions which were previously hidden are made visible, traceable, obvious.[73] Adults used to miss a lot of these. There's less excuse for missing them now.

But there are still too many people, notably politicians but also a number of parents and educators, who, in the face of all the evidence to the contrary, insist on seeing the net as a cause rather than a symptom. They prefer to disengage from it, leaving it up to technicians and technology (with the backing of police and judges) to look after kids. The kids themselves tell us that doesn't work. Holly Doel-Mackaway of Save the Children reports: 'A lot of children have written to me saying that a filter is not the solution, but they would like more information on how to deal with cyber-bullying'.[74] Tom Wood, who cracked the Howard Government's filter, told journalists: 'Filters aren't addressing the bigger issues anyway. Cyber bullying, educating children on how to protect themselves and their privacy are the first problems I'd fix'.[75] Kids are pleading for adults to stop delegating and get involved: put simply, to talk to them. While there are some encouraging educational initiatives underway, they're drowned out in public conversation by vote-grabbing rhetoric about porn, predators and filters. What will it take to get more adults, especially politicians, to really listen, either to researchers or to the kids themselves?[76]

Switching off

It's plain to see that, while digital technologies may be very empowering, there's a panoply of risks associated with them. Many of these risks are social rather than technological and require social and educational interventions. But could it be that sometimes the very state of being online is, in itself, harmful? And, if so, what might an appropriate educational intervention look like?

'Welcome to the always-on world', wrote Phil Agre in 2001.[77] 'Since there is no "class" per se, there's always class', one educator told Gene Maeroff, as he reported in 2003.[78] 'If you have your phone with you, you're effectively "logged on"', wrote Leonard Low on his blog in 2007.[79] We never switch off. And unsurprisingly, our communications technologies have begun to overwhelm us. Although many of the terms we hear – 'information overload', 'information fatigue syndrome', 'news fatigue', 'infomania', 'information obesity' and even 'infobesity'[80] – focus on the informational aspects of the problem, it's arguably more of a 'communication overload'. There are countless communication channels through which both informational and social messages can reach us: we're drowning in overlapping RSS feeds, tweets, Facebook updates, instant messages, text messages and emails, yet we keep adding more channels. One study suggests knowledge workers get as little as three minutes at a time uninterrupted, with 'switching costs' meaning that time is constantly lost as we shift back and forth between different tasks, often focusing on immediate, minor issues and leaving ourselves little time for extended reflection on important tasks.[81] More and more, technology functions as a wireless yoke to the workplace, from which we never entirely disconnect.[82] Meanwhile, constant connectivity to friends and family, while reassuring, undermines our independence and never leaves us alone with our own thoughts. Work and leisure blur together: we're available 24/7 for one or other or both.

The search for workplace solutions is being spearheaded by the Information Overload Research Group (IORG), including representatives from IBM, Intel and Microsoft. Some Silicon Valley companies have instituted 'topless meetings' (without laptops) while other businesses have experimented, albeit not very successfully, with email-free days. It may be that social networking or microblogging technologies, whose ambient communication streams don't demand constant engagement, offer a partial solution, although they can be addictive in their own ways. But perhaps this is another area where the younger generation is a step ahead, being more adept at taming the technology so that it limits who has access to them, and when.[83] iPods and iPhones, for example, can be used to insulate you from interactions with other people, whether strangers on the bus or colleagues across the room. Text messages can be substituted for conversations you'd rather not have verbally. The jury is still out, though, on the long-term consequences of keeping strangers and colleagues at arm's length or relegating difficult subjects (and difficult people) to text-only formats.

Some of the most productive strategies for dealing with tech overload may not involve technology itself: while it won't help with personal communications, we can benefit from the mediation of information by librarians, critics and journalists, as noted earlier. Yes, we may reserve the right to get second (third, fourth) opinions from the blogosphere or YouTube, but trusted experts do us an enormous service in sifting through the vast quantity of information, reducing it to a digestible amount, and annotating and commenting on it. That's exactly why there's such an intense hunt for expert Twitterers to follow! Likewise, while the idea of educating yourself from the net has a certain romantic appeal, there's little doubt the process can be both greatly streamlined and enormously enriched with the guidance of a teacher, especially one who is both a subject expert and pedagogically informed.

But perhaps the most commonly adopted response to information and communication overload, if not necessarily the best one, is multitasking. The clearest evidence comes from research on media consumption. While TV watching is noticeably declining among net users,[84] an even more striking trend shows people squeezing in more and more beyond saturation point; 61 per cent of Australian net users, for example, say they watch TV while online, with 50 per cent listening to the radio.[85] Similar trends are found in the UK and US.[86] It's not uncommon to see today's students juggling their iPhones, iPods and iMacs while chatting to friends with the TV on in the background. Multitasking may be a useful adaptive strategy in a digitally infused environment, as

"While I'm sending e-mail, trading stocks, and communicating with clients, my feet are just wasting time! What have you got to make my feet more productive?"

Figure 4.3. Multitasking mania. Cartoon © Randy Glasbergen, 2001, <www.glasbergen.com>.

Henry Jenkins has argued:

> Multi-tasking and attention should not be seen as oppositional forces. Rather, we should think of them as two complementary skills, both strategically employed by the brain to intelligently manage constraints on short-term memory.[87]

But that doesn't mean there isn't a downside. Our attention is finite. Unless we're talking about perceptions or automated actions, we humans just aren't cut out for parallel processing – so multitasking in fact means toggling very rapidly between different tasks. Laboratory results are clear: on tasks with similar cognitive demands, this leads to a loss of speed and accuracy as well as degrading recall.[88] While there may be advantages in terms of lateral thinking, there's a real danger of our thinking becoming shallow and even 'staccato', as experienced blogger Bruce Friedman suggests,[89] if we fail to take the time to reflect more deeply or weave connections between bite-sized thoughts. That may impact on many areas of our personal and professional lives, cutting us off permanently from Csikszentmihalyi's elusive state of flow,[90] and is a real quandary for education. It's a recipe, too, for a continuing increase in attention disorders, not to mention rising stress levels.

Linda Stone, a former vice-president of Microsoft, suggests we now live in a state of 'continuous partial attention'. In other words, we pay full attention to nothing and partial attention to everything as we desperately try to avoid missing anything important. This leads to 'an artificial sense of crisis' accompanied by 'over-stimulation and lack of fulfillment'. She goes on:

> I believe attention is the most powerful tool of the human spirit. We can enhance or augment our attention with practices like meditation and exercise, diffuse it with technologies like email and Blackberries or alter it with pharmaceuticals. In the end, though, we are fully responsible for how we choose to use this extraordinary tool.[91]

So maybe it's time to take a step back. Kevin Kelly, founding Executive Editor of *Wired*, has described a 'neo-Amish' attitude to technology, whereby people assess its value in any given context.[92] Legal scholar Lawrence Lessig gets 'off the grid' on annual holidays.[93] Social networking researcher danah boyd takes an 'email sabbatical'.[94] Stone herself recommends that we 'find the OFF switch on our devices, now and then'.[95] These are people at the peak of the technology game. They're not rejecting technology but recommending we use it less obsessively. That means taking breaks from it once in a while so we can slow down – which, at the same time, gives us the chance to pause and take in the bigger picture. The book you're reading right now was conceived in a seaside villa with no telephone or internet connection, but with a balcony where I could sit and watch the sun set and the moon rise over the ocean…and take the time to think at length. Sometimes, we need to remove ourselves from the constant pull of technology to find the mental space to think productively *about* technology and how it fits into our lives.

In the end, it's about balance. That's very important in education. Students need to experience the benefits of combining fast(-er) communication with slow(-er) reflection. While it's true that social constructivism and collaborative pedagogies de-emphasise solitary thought in favour of interaction, they do so to redress a previous imbalance; we'd be foolish to allow a fixation on technology to unbalance the equation the other way. Quick online searches and near-instantaneous communication facilitate some aspects of education, while more considered activities, from traditional essay writing to the building of PLEs and e-portfolios, facilitate others. Balance is also important in identity building. The net gives us great narrative freedom but it can take it away, too, and one of the ways it does so is to rob us of the time and composure to think carefully about the self or selves we are crafting. And balance is important to our biology. Ironically, the highly educated knowledge workers who were the first to see the value of switching on the new technology have also been the first to see the value – to their health, mental wellbeing, and integrated understanding of the world – in switching it off from time to time. It would be unforgivable if analogue-only evenings, breaks and holidays were to become little more than a fashionable hobby of the elites.

Looking through a social lens makes it clear that digital technologies place demands on educators which go well beyond what we saw through a pedagogical lens. We have to coach students in the digital competencies which will give them narrative control as they craft their online identities, build their social networks and compose their life stories. We have to provide guidance and mentoring in areas of personal and social risk, from cyberbullying to cybersurveillance. And we have to help them understand when and why to turn off their monitors and mobiles, so that an inability to switch off doesn't end up becoming yet another marker of the digital divide.

5

Many stories

A sociopolitical lens

Watching young people use mobile phones in Tokyo and Helsinki at the turn of the millennium, Howard Rheingold sensed he'd glimpsed the future.[1] I have a similar sense that I've caught glimpses of the digital future: in the astonishing clockwork precision of Dubai and Tokyo, but equally in the breathtaking hi-tech, low-tech juxtapositions of Hong Kong and Chennai. What struck Rheingold were the synergies between Tokyo and Helsinki. They're certainly there; but I'm equally struck by the differences. It strikes me, for example, that the future I'm glimpsing doesn't always look very Western. And it strikes me that the future looks slightly different – and sometimes startlingly different – for different people in different places.

Yes, there are common issues around the world. But there are also differences. Everyone, everywhere, fits technology into their own stories. What people make of its affordances in diverse geographical, social and political contexts can turn it into an instrument of equality or stratification, individualism or collectivism, freedom or oppression. Of course it's a two-way process: our stories influence our uptake of technology, but technology in turn impacts on our individual, community and national stories. Some people want to use digital technologies to alter old stories or write new ones. Others see ways of using the same technologies to reinforce old stories. Some of these stories are already in conflict with each other and others soon will be. Some of the conflicts will play themselves out in courts of law, some at the ballot box, and others in prisons and torture chambers. The possible outcomes are as varied as the human beings who compose the stories and the technologies they use to shape and share them.

Old divisions, new divisions
The West divided

In February 2008, a video made by four white students at the University of the Free State in South Africa was widely circulated on the net. It showed the students directing elderly black cleaning staff to drink beer and attempt athletic tasks, and it ended with one of the students apparently urinating on food in secret before giving it to the workers to eat, making them ill. The video, it seems, was made in protest at racial integration on campus.[2] The same year, in Australia's Northern Territory, a police officer filmed a drunk Aborigine who was instructed to sing and dance for the camera. The video was uploaded to an adult entertainment site and subsequently found its way onto YouTube.[3] Typically, old stories of inequality get reinscribed in new media. It's only our historical blindness that allows us to think otherwise: to think that each new communications technology will automatically herald a new era of democracy and social justice. On the net, we regularly witness the ritual humiliation of non-dominant ethnicities and sexualities; we find disabled users underrepresented, giving lie to the notion of the 'disembodiment' of cyberspace;[4] and we see the reinscription of class through social networking, with Facebook and MySpace, for example, diverging along socioeconomic lines.[5]

On the other hand, in a recent post-Blairite assault on elitism, the British House of Lords has experimented with YouTube videos to engage youth as well as setting up a blogging initiative called *Lords of the Blog,* designed to 'encourage direct dialogue between web users across the world and Members of the House of Lords'.[6] The affordances of web 2.0 mean that there is real democratic potential in both blogs and YouTube, but it's up to us to make something of that potential. And that means addressing the issue of the digital divide, which is about more than technology. After all, for a member of the public to engage effectively in dialogue with a British Lord takes far more than an internet connection: it needs a sophisticated combination of traditional and digital literacies.

Overcoming the digital divide, then, firstly requires broadening access to the internet, whether through computers and broadband networks as in many developed countries, or through the expansion of wireless mobile technologies, perhaps linked to cloud computing, as is gradually happening in both developed and developing parts of the world. Secondly, it requires broadening access to digital literacies, ranging from the search and information literacies necessary to inform and educate yourself to the participatory and communicative literacies necessary to take part in public forums. Thirdly, it requires going beyond digital connectivity and digital literacy to help users view the net through a wide range of lenses, extending their understanding of its nature and their level of control over how it fits into their lives. That might even include switching it off from time to time: at one end of the scale, overcoming the digital divide means helping people connect to the net; at the other end, it may mean helping them disconnect.

Educators can play a driving role here as long as they're not hampered by governmental or institutional restrictions. Provision of fast computers and connections in educational institutions is essential for students with limited home access. However, a narrow back-to-basics agenda which restricts how computers are used will be very damaging. While negatively impacting all students, it will mainly disadvantage those whose home environments, for technical or social reasons, don't give them the chance to acquire advanced digital literacies. School or library computing will be much less effective in compensating for a lack of home computing if access is blocked to key social networking and social sharing sites: the very places kids from wealthier backgrounds are busy building the online identities and social networks which will serve them well in the future. And teachers will only be able to help students contextualise digital technologies, weaving them into the stories of their own lives, if both teachers and students can access the full gamut of web 2.0 and related tools.

Finally, if offline intolerance and discrimination are reproducing themselves online – and they are – there's a strong argument for promoting universal digital literacy as part of a broader social justice agenda. It comes back to lenses. Students must learn to view the net itself as well as their online activities not just through technological or pedagogical lenses, but through social and sociopolitical lenses as well. Our best hope of combating the viral spread of abusive videos of black South Africans or Australian Aborigines is to give the digital exploiters a framework for (re-)considering their actions at the same time as the digitally exploited get a right of reply.

East divided from West

'Has [the web] been designed by the West for the West?' asked its founder, Tim Berners-Lee, rhetorically in 2008.[7] Ghostly colonial patterns are re-emerging: 'below the metaphoric surface of the cyber-planet, are people who cook, clean, build and work without the benefits of digi-leisure'.[8] Few of them are in the West. Few of them, whatever their age, are what Prensky had in mind when he coined the term 'digital natives'. Some of them are in fact online, like those working 10 or 12-hour shifts in Chinese sweatshops acquiring virtual goods to sell to wealthy online gamers (a practice called 'gold farming') or levelling up the latter's game characters (known as 'power levelling'). Others may never see the net, like the kids searching for saleable parts in first-world computer dumps in Nigeria, poisoning themselves with toxic chemicals as they do so.

The net has become such an integral part of global affairs that those who can't use it effectively will struggle to make their stories heard. In fact there are already plenty of voices from developing countries in cyberspace, but most belong to a cosmopolitan minority:

> Most Kenyans spend idle afternoons discussing technology in trendy cafes. Nearly all Venezuelans oppose Chavez. And throughout the Middle East you'd be hard pressed to find anyone who supports sharia law. Or, at least, those would be your impressions of the world as shaped by the ever-expanding global blogosphere. As much as participatory media have democratized how we find out about the world around us, the new global voices tend to come from a narrow demographic: highly educated, urban, and upper-middle class.[9]

When it comes to the international digital divide, technologically enhanced education has played and continues to play an ambiguous role. Its benefits in developing countries have, so far, been mainly reserved for the above-mentioned elites. It's true that more and more non-Westerners are coming online thanks to wireless mobile telephony, though we have to remember that many mobile phones lack extensive functionality, are non-generative, and may be prohibitively expensive to use. On the other hand, there are promising initiatives like the One Laptop Per Child (OLPC) project, which is specifically aimed at overcoming the digital divide through education, by making low-cost, networked laptops available to young learners in poor or deprived contexts.

But infrastructure and equipment are just the start. Once learners are online, cultural issues loom large. Although OLPC takes a more culturally inclusive approach, the international computing landscape is still dominated by Western corporate iconography. What does a manila folder mean to someone who's never seen an office? What does a recycling bin mean to someone who lives on less than a dollar a day? And while learners in much of the world may benefit from the growing linguistic and cultural diversification of the net, as mentioned earlier, English retains a powerful position, both as the macrolanguage which binds together the network of linguistic patches and as the lingua franca of transnational education. Initiatives ranging from the Creative Commons to Open Educational Resources may help overcome the digital divide in terms of access to online resources, but even when material is linguistically and culturally accessible (Wikipedia, for example, is now available in more than 260 languages), countries like China are starting to shut their citizens off from this common human cultural production as they insulate themselves from the global net,[10] partly to enforce security and surveillance, and partly to resist the perceived onslaught of Western digital cultural imperialism.

And here's the rub. When Diana Kleiner, Director of the Open Yale Courses, stated in 2008 that '[i]t seems to us that a university like [Yale] has a responsibility to continue to democratise knowledge',[11] she hit the nail on the head. For Western institutions are exporting a lot more than course materials. We're exporting a notion of democracy and, with it, a whole philosophy of rationality and individualism based in Western modernity. This becomes especially problematic when, rather than just providing open access to materials, we start to sign students up for the international online courses increasingly offered by Western institutions.

Leaving aside questions of access, and even language, we demand a lot of participants on international courses. When, for example, we ask students to join asynchronous discussion forums (whose very name recalls their heritage stretching back to ancient Rome) we're asking them to position themselves as autonomous individuals who will interact as equals with both peers and teachers, challenging others' arguments and promoting their own views according to principles of rational debate. When we ask students to write blogs, we may be creating a conflict around issues of privacy and publicity for those who aren't at ease with the post-1960s Western paradigm of free self-expression. When we ask students to contribute to wikis, we could be plunging them into uncomfortable public disputes, as we saw in Chapter 3. Interestingly, in 2008 Jimmy Wales described Wikipedia as 'the online encyclopedia in which any *reasonable* person can join us in writing and editing entries on any encyclopedic topic [emphasis added]'.[12] A culturally neutral definition of 'reasonable', anyone? And that goes for subcultures within the West as much as for non-Westerners. Even with the most laudable intentions there are plenty of potential educational pitfalls, ranging from students misunderstanding expectations to educators imposing a monolithic academic literacy.

Less laudable, however, are the effects of the commodification and marketisation of education, which is sometimes seen, in itself, as a new phase of neocolonialism. Qualifications become commodities; courses become packages; and students become customers. This imposes a very particular, very narrow Western perspective on learning. So, although we need to recognise the dangers of the cultural assumptions which underpin more constructivist or democratic Western educational exports, it would be even more remiss of us to sit back and allow those with fewer frissons of conscience to impose a commodity paradigm of education. If we're exporting Western education, let's export the best of what we have to offer. Ultimately, as Martha McCormick recognises:

> It may be that there is no way to share technology and, at the same time, be so culturally relativist as to avoid any imposition of the values of the cultures providing the technologies. There may be no fail-safe way to provide the technological vehicles of communication without their also becoming, in a sense, ideological overseers of that communication.[13]

But we can at least act with cultural sensitivity. We can aim for balance in our materials, perspectives and practices. And we should bear in mind that teachers, too, have much to learn. The greatest potential in bringing diverse peoples together on the net surely lies in the chance to communicate with and learn from each other. The statements below come from participants in multicultural discussion forums for language teachers which I organised or co-organised in 2006–2007:

> [W]ith students from different backgrounds and exposure to other cultures, there was much sharing of ideas and perspectives – things that I may never have come across in books, but only through the sharing of personal experiences of others.

> The 'classroom' as a concept goes beyond the four walls of a room – this on-line discussion is a good platform for the exchange of views around the world – it is an opportunity for multi-directional learning to take place.[14]

When such interactions go well, the result can be a kind of 'epistemological humility',[15] a recognition that your way of seeing the world is not the only way – and that you can learn from and about others who have different ways of seeing the world. It's about the shift from *must* to *might,* writ large. But whether the net helps us acquire this kind of epistemological humility depends very much on how it's used.

The message in Figure 5.1 was posted on the web in March 2008 after the LiveLeak video sharing service took down *Fitna,* a video about Islam by Geert Wilders, a right-wing Dutch politician. The video was subsequently reinstated but not until after LiveLeak had taken security measures to protect its staff who, it said, had received serious threats. Similarly, when the first Muslim virtual world, Muxlim Pal, launched in beta in December 2008, it had to be closed within hours due to 'griefer' attacks. It, too, was quickly reinstated, albeit with temporary restrictions on access by new members. There's no easy answer here. Contact between individuals or groups doesn't automatically lead to acceptance and appreciation, or collaboration and collective intelligence. It can entrench differences and deepen divisions. The net has brought some 1.5 billion people into (potential) contact with each other and that number will grow in coming years. This raises the spectre of serious conflict which can spill over into cyberterrorism as well as offline threats.

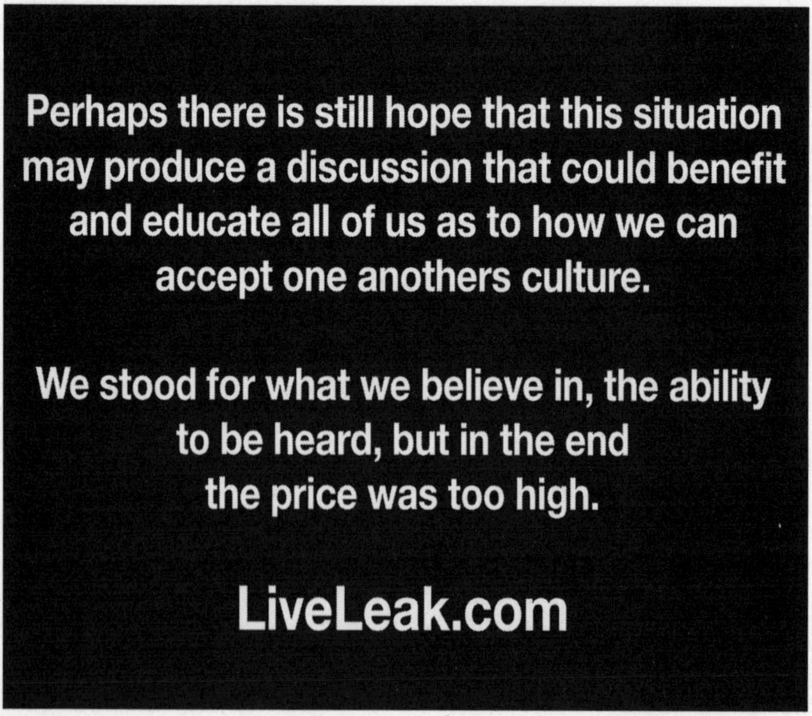

> **Perhaps there is still hope that this situation may produce a discussion that could benefit and educate all of us as to how we can accept one anothers culture.**
>
> **We stood for what we believe in, the ability to be heard, but in the end the price was too high.**
>
> **LiveLeak.com**

Figure 5.1. Intercultural clashes. Message posted at LiveLeak.com after the removal of the Fitna video.

Given the clashes which can arise from unmediated intercultural encounters, there's an urgent need for education to prepare students – as many as we can get online, and as quickly as we can get them online – through mediated experiences. Students may be able to develop intercultural literacy as they encounter human diversity (what postmodernists might call 'Otherness') in carefully constructed, and constructivist, learning spaces.[16] With capable teachers as facilitators and mentors, they could start to engage with diverse others; discuss diverse cultural perspectives; and perhaps come to understand that different individuals and different societies tell different stories, and that difference doesn't always necessitate a backlash. How reason stacks up against faith, or the global against the local, is unclear. But whatever the limitations of Western discussion forums, blogs or wikis, and however culturally sensitive we must be when inducting students into such spaces, their promise – of words instead of weapons, or, if need be, words as weapons rather than bombs as weapons – has value. It's better, as Jimmy Wales says, to disagree in safety. This is an odd alignment, perhaps, of the rational heritage of the Enlightenment with the liberating ethos of the 60s. But it may well be the best of what Western education has to offer in a rapidly globalising world.

Beyond states and markets
Voices in the halls of power
In 2008, during the media blackout ahead of the Chinese Olympic torch run to the summit of Mount Everest, bloggers on the mountain still managed to get their messages out.[17] In Cuba, blogger Yoani Sánchez has long been a thorn in the side of the government regime with her open net presence.[18] In Saudi Arabia, where women make up half of all bloggers, men and women are using chatrooms to relate in ways they cannot in public.[19] In the UAE, female students have been known to swap their abayas for bling in Second Life.[20] Korean girls have reported finding freedom from traditional gender roles in online games.[21] Facebook has been used by young people in Australia to amplify resistance to proposed net censorship laws, and by citizens of the UK to protest their government's proposed monitoring of social networking sites – like Facebook![22] Everywhere, it's getting harder to silence the voices of difference and dissent.

The rise of 'citizen journalism' means that news from around the world is instantly available in undigested form, usually before reporters are even on the scene: think of the Flickr photos of the London bombings in 2005, the blogged images of the Burmese military crackdown in 2007, or the Twitter postings from the scene of the Mumbai bombings in 2008.

But it also means the availability of a far wider range of commentary: in the West, blogs came into their own as an alternative to the mainstream media at the time of the second Iraq War.[23] The essence of citizen journalism is perhaps best captured by South Korea's groundbreaking online newspaper, *OhmyNews,* with its slogan 'Every citizen is a reporter'. At its extreme, citizen journalism may even blur into remix culture, with young people expressing their views of current events in the form of sophisticated multimodal parodies. Here, journalistic commentary meets artistic commentary: Dadaism gone global.

Associated with citizen journalism, we're seeing the rise of 'sousveillance', or observation from below. Singer Peter Gabriel, founder of WITNESS, an organisation established in 1992 to promote the use of video in human rights advocacy, has spoken about 'little brothers' and 'little sisters' watching Big Brother.[24] There's no doubt the communicative potential of today's web 2.0 tools makes the task of sousveillance immeasurably easier than it was in 1992. And it can have major and immediate consequences. A US policeman, dubbed the 'Baltimore Cop', was disciplined after it came to light that he'd assaulted a skater kid – while being secretly filmed by one of the victim's friends using a mobile

Figure 5.2. Voices being heard. Blog Action Day 2008. Image by Collis Ta'eed. Used with permission.

phone.[25] An American journalism student detained while covering a demonstration in Egypt used Twitter to post an initial one-word message – 'arrested' – and, thanks to his Twitter followers and the US Embassy, found himself released the next day.[26] Wikileaks, a web service which allows whistleblowers from anywhere in the world to anonymously publish sensitive governmental or corporate materials, already hosts well over a million such documents.

In recent years, we've also seen the dramatic effects of 'smart mobs' or 'flash mobs', crystallising almost instantaneously around shared causes with the help of digital technologies.[27] All involved young, digitally literate people using technology to organise mass protests or campaigns. All primarily involved communication between individuals as opposed to broadcast communication. Thus, mobile phones and the internet played a key role in the overthrow of Philippines President Joseph Estrada in 2001; as they did in the last-minute reversal of the electoral fortunes of Roh Moo-Hyun, leading to his election as President of South Korea in 2002; and in the overthrow of Spain's right-wing Partido Popular in the wake of the Madrid bombings in 2004.[28] Maybe, indeed, incumbent governments are right to be uneasy about the spread of these technologies. At the time of going to press in July 2009, it appeared that Twitter and other social media had helped facilitate the post-election protests that briefly destabilised Iranian politics, while protests by Chinese net users seemed to have been instrumental in effecting a rare (though perhaps temporary) backdown by the Chinese Government over its proposed mandatory installation of 'Green Dam Youth Escort' anti-pornography software on new computers.[29] How these and other similar situations will play out over coming years remains to be seen – but there's a sense of new possibilities in the air.

On a more mundane level, but one which may turn out to have greater long-term effects than one-off political revolts, we're seeing more regular involvement of ordinary citizens in the day-to-day politics of their communities and countries. Some states have been quick to respond to a perceived need to interact more closely with their citizens: in the US, you've long been able to befriend politicians on Facebook or MySpace; in the UK, you can petition the government on the Number 10 website or complain about local problems at FixMyStreet; in Australia, you can follow the Prime Minister or Leader of the Opposition on Twitter (with the curious and somewhat disconcerting consequence that both will, in turn, sign up to follow you...). Even President Ahmadinejad of Iran has a blog, if a little-used one, and did so ahead of any US president![30]

But the significance of such channels, especially when uncomprehending politicians try to use them for broadcasting purposes, pales in comparison with the burgeoning culture of online activism. Speaking on OneWebDay in 2008, Lawrence Lessig proclaimed: 'It is time the virtual gets used to fix the real'.[31] The process is already underway. In coming years, we can expect to see more and more offline interventions using online spaces as a springboard. Some represent grassroots initiatives but, interestingly, many operate on a hybrid model where digital activists use spaces set up or supported by major organisations, including commercial ones. Amid early signs of a rising culture of youth civic activism, John Palfrey and Urs Gasser propose that the transformation of politics by networked activists may turn out to be the net's most important effect.[32]

A random but representative list of promising initiatives might include the social change platform Change.org; the citizen media project Global Voices and its outreach arm, Rising Voices, whose slogan is: 'Helping the global population join the global conversation'; the annual Blog Action Day, which in 2008 focused on raising awareness of poverty (Figure 5.2); the MySpace Impact Awards and the Facebook for Good contest; the Rock the Vote site, which offers young US citizens tools for political engagement; the UK Channel 4/Bebo site Battlefront, designed to inspire youth to see the net 'as a canvas for social change'[33]; the OECD FutureInternet Channel where, in the lead-up to a 2008 ministerial meeting in Seoul, YouTube users were invited to submit videos giving their ideas on 'how the Internet can improve the world'[34]; or the USC Network Culture Project's 2008 Second Life and the Public Good Community Challenge, which asked participants to propose ways of using the virtual world to benefit the public good. Second Life, with its large nonprofit presence, is a field leader, hosting sites ranging from the International Justice Center to Union Island, and events ranging from the Second Life Human Rights Festival to the Relay for Life of Second Life. In 2009 it offered an inaugural Linden Prize for an 'inworld project that improves the way people work, learn and communicate in their daily lives outside of the virtual world'.[35] As Chris Anderson has noted, the web (and, we might add, the net in general) gives altruism 'a platform where the actions of individuals can have global impact'.[36]

There is real potential in ordinary people using technology to help them rework old stories and write new ones. There's potential for the expression of individual voices, the advancement of coordinated social interventions, and the development of an engaged citizenry. There's educational potential, too: to learn *about* political engagement, to learn *through* civic engagement, and to learn that both are open, not just to pre-digital organisations or lobby groups, but to anyone who is digitally literate. In particular, teachers can lower some of the barriers between educational institutions and wider society by introducing students to social initiatives on discussion boards, blogs and wikis, or to online communities which can provide inspiration and models for future civic involvement. But, as we'll see shortly, none of this potential will be realised unless we can convince our increasingly jittery governments to refrain from clamping down on networking technologies as they attempt to reassert their influence over an ever more unruly digital landscape.

Voices in the marketplace

Have you ever received an email invitation to share in the fortune of an exiled Nigerian Government minister in return for a small favour? As you're probably well aware, you're not the only one. Email scamming is rumoured to have become one of Nigeria's largest industries. Responding to Australian media reports on the situation, the Nigerian High Commissioner to Australia recently recommended that victims of Nigerian email fraud should themselves be jailed – for greed.[37] There's little doubt that the internet is very much bound up with money and all the frailties and oddities that accompany its pursuit in a global marketplace.

Naturally, the net is also home to a great deal of legitimate commerce. It didn't take long for entrepreneurs to see the business potential of Berners-Lee's world wide web. That potential has exceeded the wildest dreams of many. In 2005, MySpace was bought by Rupert Murdoch's

"I've outsourced my job to a dog overseas who will be your companion via web cam."

Figure 5.3. Global markets. Cartoon © Randy Glasbergen, 2004, <www.glasbergen.com>.

News Corp for US $580 million. In 2006, YouTube was bought by Google for US $1.65 billion. The same year, Anshe Chung became the first Second Life resident to acquire US $1 million in virtual assets. Mark Zuckerberg, creator of Facebook, became the youngest billionaire in the Forbes Rich List in 2008 (though he disappeared from it in 2009). Each year from 2007 to 2009, Google has been named the number one brand in the world in the BrandZ Top 100. Notwithstanding the shock of the global financial crisis which began in 2008, commercial interests will inevitably continue to exert a strong influence on the web 2.0 landscape. In this context, numerous commentators have expressed concern over the ways companies are shaping the consumer identities of young technology users[38] or the civic spaces of virtual worlds.[39] And while the world's poor find themselves slavishly tilling virtual gold farms, more affluent youth on the other side of the digital divide find technology companies reaping the profits of the unpaid labour they put into the creation and sharing of UGC.[40]

Yet there are some young users who are managing to make their voices heard in the marketplace. 'The age of gerontocracy is over', announced Palfrey and Gasser in 2008:[41] thanks to the internet, which can dramatically reduce the cost of going into business, young people have more opportunity than at any time in history to turn their ideas and energy into commercial successes along the lines demonstrated by Zuckerberg at Facebook. Of course, the 'strong techno-libertarian streak' of the founders of many web 2.0 startup companies[42] helps them capitalise (and not just metaphorically) on the 60s ethos of the whole webscape. Younger business leaders 'get' the notion of the produser in a way older leaders often don't. They know that their users will expect to contribute, sometimes for financial reward, more often not; that they'll expect to be able to personalise technologies, remix cultural products and mash up software; that they'll expect to have a voice and use it to share their ideas, their views, their remixes and their mashups; and that they'll expect to do so within a growing social community. Nor will they necessarily care if someone, somewhere, is skimming off a profit as long as that someone, somewhere, continues to provide the infrastructure for the online community. This is a culture where, as readers told Charles Leadbeater, 'you are what you share'. He goes on to explain:

In the economy of things you are identified by what you own – your land, house, car. In the economy of ideas that the web is creating, you are what you share – who you are linked to, who you network with and which ideas, pictures, videos, links or comments you share.[43]

Many firms, old and new, are exploring ways of adapting to the new landscape: contributing to open source projects, freely giving away basic products, interacting directly with their customers, providing channels for the latter to connect with each other, and venturing into the area of social commerce. None of this means the death of corporations or markets. It may however signal the rise of new business models and 'a new kind of ecological capitalism, wherein corporate interests are intertwined with the interests of customers, suppliers, and even competitors'.[44] That is, if countervailing tendencies towards surveillance, censorship and copyright litigation don't get in the way. Such tendencies, as we'll see, could undermine the emerging ecosystem, reducing or eliminating the benefits consumers, produsers, educators or students might hope to draw from the web 2.0 marketplace and its many free software products and interactive forums.

States, markets and networks

In all of the above, the big news is the arrival of technologies which support the fast creation and easy maintenance of networks of people who choose to cooperate and collaborate without coercion by states or markets (or the companies that operate within markets) and without the constraints of hierarchies or formal rules. And it *is* big news. Networks are an important alternative form of social organisation:

> For the last hundred years the big organizational question has been whether any given task was best taken on by the state, directing the effort in a planned way, or by businesses competing in a market. This debate was based on the universal and unspoken supposition that people couldn't simply self-assemble; the choice between markets and managed effort assumed that there was no third alternative. Now there is. Our electronic networks are enabling novel forms of collective action, enabling the creation of collaborative groups that are larger and more distributed than at any other time in history. The scope of work that can be done by noninstitutional groups is a profound challenge to the status quo.[45]

So Clay Shirky explains it, highlighting the sociopolitical ramifications. Yochai Benkler makes a similar point with an economic twist, referring specifically to markets and companies: 'It is a mistake to think that we have only two basic free transactional forms – property-based markets and hierarchically organized firms. We have three, and the third is social sharing and exchange'.[46] And thanks to digital networks, that kind of sharing and exchange is now possible on a large scale.

Of course, networks are not a new form of social organisation, since they've long underpinned extended families and local communities. What's new is the size and scope of the networks which can be built and maintained with the aid of digital technologies, and the impact they may therefore have on the politics of states and the economics of markets (not to mention their facilitation of participatory culture, distributed education or online socialisation). It's not a question of replacement, however. If networks can exist alongside states and markets, they may act as a corrective to some of the extremes to which state-based and market-based organisation can lead. But states and markets are also important correctives to each other, and indeed to networks. States in particular may act as a corrective to the limitations of networks: after all, how large can a self-organising group become before structures of authority are needed? States may also act as a corrective to the excesses of networks: we need to remember that networks benefit terrorists and paedophiles as much as they benefit social activists or sexual minorities. In fact, it's largely terrorists and paedophiles – or, in the non-Western variation, terrorists and pornographers – who have given states the moral platform they feel they need to begin reining in the free voices of the net.

Patrolling every/body

'The wild colt of new technologies can and must be controlled', said the Cuban Communications Minister Ramiro Valdes in 2007,[47] expressing a sentiment shared by many undemocratic regimes – and ever larger numbers of democratic ones. More and more, states are (re-)imposing old geographic borders on the once borderless net, as indeed they must in order to exert control. After all, states' influence on the net depends less on their virtual than their physical prowess; it depends on the fact that there are, everywhere, bodies behind computer screens. Bodies located in real territories. Political bodies, social bodies and sexual bodies. Bodies that can be tracked and, if need be, punished.

Certainly, states have cause for concern. We've already seen the precursors of cyberwarfare: the Russian denial of service attacks on Estonia in 2007 or Georgia in 2008,[48] and the overflow into cyberspace of the Sunni–Shi'ite conflict in the Gulf or the Israeli–Palestinian conflict in Gaza.[49] It's not only about cyberterrorism, of course, but about technology's role in the coordination and carrying out of attacks like those which have taken place in New York, Bali, Madrid, London and Mumbai. Thomas Friedman, author of the seminal *The World is Flat*, puts it this way:

The playing field is not being leveled only in ways that draw in and superempower a whole new group of innovators. It's being leveled in a way that draws in and superempowers a whole new group of angry, frustrated, and humiliated men and women.[50]

Then there are the net's self-appointed social and moral vigilantes, ranging from Western groups bent on vengeance of one kind or another to China's human flesh search engines. There's venomous e-hate: racism, sexism and homophobia spread virally online. There are alarming cases of identity theft and financially motivated cybercrime. And there's the scourge of child pornography.

Without a doubt, the internet has its dark and unpleasant corners, some of which represent genuine dangers and demand the vigilance of governments, intelligence organisations and law enforcement agencies. But the greater danger may be that states – including the supposedly democratic ones – are reacting to perceived dangers in an increasingly authoritarian way, intensifying surveillance while undermining civil liberties and democratic accountability in the name of security,[51] morality, or both. In the process, states of all kinds are finding their interests oddly compatible with those of companies.[52] In the last chapter, we discussed the dangers of individuals generating data about themselves or other individuals. But individuals' ability to generate data trails is nothing compared to that of governments or corporations, especially to the extent that the latter can pin unitary identities on those they are tracking. And it's in these moments, when politics and commerce collude, that the emerging freedoms of digital culture are most endangered. It may turn out that we're not as free to use the new technologies to make our voices heard, and to rewrite our individual and collective stories, as our inherited constitutions or daily lifestyles have lulled us into believing.

Surveillance

The same networks that can be used for activism and resistance can also be used by governments for surveillance and information gathering. As one Shanghai-based net entrepreneur notes: 'for the first time in China's history the central government has a popular and relatively easy means of eavesdropping on what is happening and being said in the country'.[53] Indeed, states everywhere are watching – and catching – and punishing. In 2008, for the first time, there were more online journalists than print journalists imprisoned around the world.[54]

In the developed world, there's long been a presumption of online anonymity, which has formed the basis for freely travelling the net. While the cover of anonymity allows cowardly net trolls to give full rein to their spite and makes it easier for cybermobs to form, the privacy which comes from anonymity may well be crucial to identity development and, more broadly, to democracy itself:

> [P]rivacy allows limited social experimentation – the deviations from social norms that are much riskier to the individual in the glare of public exposure, but which can be, and often have been in the past, the leading edges of progressive social changes.[55]

For both personal and social reasons, then, anonymity is vital to exploration and experimentation online. But everywhere there are moves to limit this. For example, in April 2009, in the name of counterterrorism, the UK Government implemented an EU directive allowing it to log all its citizens' emails and other net usage, adding this information to pre-existing logs of phone usage; it planned to eventually also log social networking site interactions in its '"big brother" database', as *The Times* called it. In late April, in reaction to protests, the government shifted to proposing decentralised storage of such data by ISPs.[56] In the same month, South Korea's government, having previously complained of the circulation of 'false information [...] prompting social unrest', brought in a law requiring real-name registration for Koreans wishing to post files or comment on sites with over 100,000 daily visitors.[57]

Corporate surveillance in the West largely takes the form of recording 'clickstreams' (everything a user clicks on when browsing the net) or online purchases in order to deliver better search results or more targeted advertising. Obviously, similar tracking techniques could potentially be used in the service of governments – and increasingly will be, as seen in the UK examples above. But it's outside the West that the breathtaking power of combined corporate and government surveillance can best be seen. Western companies have shown themselves only too willing to comply with local laws in other parts of the world. Most infamously, Chinese dissidents like journalist Shi Tao have found themselves with jail sentences after Yahoo! apparently complied with Chinese Government requests to hand over information about their online activities.[58] Yahoo! co-founder, Jerry Yang, professed discomfort over Shi Tao's case, but noted that 'we have to follow the law'.[59] Although, as we'll see, major technology companies have shifted their position a little in recent years, it's worth pausing to consider how technology providers will act, or feel compelled to act, as states around the world gradually tighten their surveillance laws.

State censorship

Surveillance can of course lead to censorship, including self-censorship, but censorship frequently takes much more direct forms. There's a regular flood of news reports about the on-again, off-again blocking of websites and services like Blogger or YouTube at moments of crisis in countries ranging from Armenia and Bangladesh to Pakistan and Turkey. In 2008, Thailand announced plans to build a multimillion dollar firewall to protect its king from online insults, which would give it the option to block terrorist and pornographic sites as well. Recent reports suggest that under the new government, installed at the end of 2008, work is continuing apace to censor material perceived as insulting to the monarchy.[60] Countries with particularly pervasive political filtering include Burma (Myanmar), Iran, Syria, Tunisia and Vietnam.[61] But, globally speaking, most net filtering pales in comparison with China's Golden Shield Project, often referred to as the Great Firewall of China. Wikipedia reports that in China access has variously been blocked to the BBC News (Chinese version), *The New York Times* and Radio Canada International (Chinese version); Amnesty International,

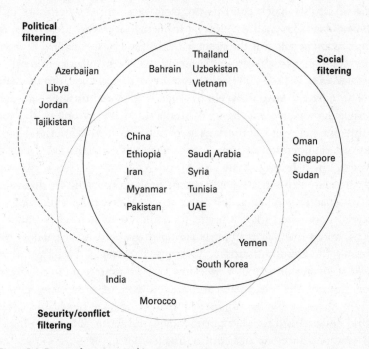

Figure 5.4. Reasons for state censorship. Image Source: Deibert, Ronald, John Palfrey, Rafal Rohozinski and Jonathan Zittrain, (eds), foreword by Janice Gross Stein, Access Denied: The Practice and Policy of Global Internet Filtering, figure 1.7: 'Content Filtering Choices', © 2008 Massachusetts Institute of Technology, by permission of The MIT Press.

Reporters Without Borders and Wikileaks; some blogging services, Flickr, Twitter, YouTube, Hotmail, iTunes...and Wikipedia itself.[62] Discussion of politically sensitive topics is not permitted. Yes, it's technically possible to use proxies or VPNs, or to talk in code, but the system of domestic censorship involves a combination of 'social control, human surveillance, peer pressure, and self-censorship'.[63] While a number of Western countries censor hate speech or materials of national concern – Germany censors Holocaust denial and neo-Nazi websites, for example[64] – broader political censorship in the West is rare.

But censorship isn't just about political material. Many states also engage in moral or social censorship. Widely differing countries from Saudi Arabia to Singapore openly advertise their censorship of pornography. In 2009, China launched a campaign to eradicate 'vulgar' material online, accusing net companies of 'violating public morality and harming the physical and mental health of youth and young people', and attempted to mandate the installation of Green Dam Youth Escort software on all new computers, as discussed earlier.[65] Again, such censorship is limited in Western countries, though many, including Canada, Denmark, Finland, Germany, Italy, New Zealand, Norway, Sweden and the UK, have in place systems whereby some or all ISPs block child pornography sites; these systems are usually voluntary and designed to prevent accidental access to illegal material.[66] While many people fear the potential expansion of such blocking to cover other content, particularly in Germany, where mandatory filtering was legislated only in June 2009,[67] the most severe dangers lie far to the south.

The current Australian Government's plan to institute nationwide internet censorship has placed Australia 'at the forefront of the spread of this practice from authoritarian regimes such as China and Iran to Western democratic nations'.[68] The Rudd Government's clean feed proposal, in a testing phase as of mid-2009, would see a two-tiered filtering system (with all the inherent limitations of filters discussed in the last chapter) applied at ISP level. It would comprise a filter covering material considered inappropriate for children, which adults could opt out of, and a mandatory filter covering illegal and, in the words of the Minister for Communications, 'unwanted' material, based on a secret blacklist of around 10,000 websites.[69] This represents a considerable expansion of the originally announced aim of protecting children. Already there have been suggestions that mandatory censorship could or should be extended to adult pornography and fetish sites, gambling sites, and even pro-anorexia and euthanasia sites.[70]

Without constitutional free speech safeguards, Australia is much more vulnerable than, say, the US or Canada to such heavy-handed government censorship,[71] making it an obvious place for this kind of experiment. Indeed, the world is watching closely for the implications of Australia's attempt to 'retrofit' censorship blocks to an open network which, unlike the Chinese or Saudi networks with their inbuilt 'choke points', was originally designed to route around such blocks.[72] The US *Blown to Bits* blog calls the plan 'absurd' but 'scary'.[73] In the UK, *The Guardian* has asked:

> What better rationale than children's sensibilities to reassure people the trampling of their rights is worth it? The Australian government's agenda on national censorship is based on an appeal to emotion – it doesn't matter what it bans or censors, it can always claim it's for the benefit of children.[74]

Wikileaks, where contested versions of the blacklist were leaked in March 2009, warns: 'History shows that secret censorship systems, whatever their original intent, are invariably corrupted into anti-democratic behavior'.[75] Within Australia, the filter is opposed by many politicians, with the Shadow Minister calling it 'misguided and deeply unpopular'[76] and one senator pointing out that '[t]he black list [...] can become very grey depending on how expansive the list becomes – euthanasia material, politically related material, material about anorexia'.[77] It's opposed by the press, with an opinion writer in *The Australian* referring to 'Book burning in the digital age'[78] and another in *The Sydney Morning Herald* warning: 'The information troglodytes are back on the attack'.[79] It's opposed by industry and IT experts.[80] It's opposed, vociferously, on Facebook, MySpace, Twitter and YouTube. It's opposed by the general public, with polls showing opposition running at 79 to 86 per cent,[81] and even by children's groups, with Save the Children calling it 'fundamentally flawed'.[82]

Faced with such opposition, the Minister reiterates the need to eradicate child porn.[83] It's unlikely any of the above opponents of the clean feed would disagree, though many would remind the Minister that, as we saw in the last chapter, web filters are largely useless in this area. Unfortunately, however, 'child porn', like 'terrorism', is easy to use as a rhetorical trump card to shut down conversation, giving socially and morally conservative governments considerable latitude to probe and police their citizens' personal lives. Australians and, in their wake, other Westerners may yet find themselves taking lessons from Chinese or Iranian dissidents on how to continue to communicate freely – and to write and rewrite their own stories – online.

Corporate censorship

Outside the West, the market has shown itself to be as amenable to censorship as to surveillance. The building of China's Great Firewall was only possible thanks to Western technologies, while Google and Microsoft have made the news in recent years over censorship in China.[84] In the West, by contrast, market censorship tends to be far more subtle: it's about what you don't see, not because you can't for legal or technical reasons, but because it's too time-consuming to look beyond the first page of results, some of them paid links, on commercial search engines; because it's too troublesome to push outside the charmed circle of the most famous blogs, which happen to belong to international media conglomerates; or because it's too inconvenient to look for photos or videos which are not hosted on the best known sharing sites.

But things are changing fast in the West. In February 2007, Stephanie Lenz posted a 29-second home video on YouTube, showing her toddler dancing to a Prince track which was heard playing faintly in the background. In June, it was removed by YouTube in accordance with a takedown notice issued by Universal Music. However, Stephanie filed a counter-notice with YouTube, which saw the video reinstated – and she then followed up by suing Universal for damages, with a judge eventually ruling that companies must take 'fair use' into account before ordering takedowns.[85] Of course, this is just one story among thousands. Many have less happy outcomes for ordinary net users. Every day, we hear about record companies suing kids who've swapped music online, broadcasters issuing takedown notices for program excerpts appearing on video sharing sites, or lawsuits being brought against bloggers.

Copyright law, with its origins in the 1709 Statute of Anne, is designed to strike a balance between the rights of creators (to encourage them to keep creating) and the rights of the public (to make use of creative works, especially those they've purchased).[86] In recent years, the balance in many jurisdictions has shifted dramatically in favour of creators so that copyright law functions increasingly as a protector of market interests, in particular those of the large companies which came to dominate most cultural production in the twentieth century. Many of these companies, whose profit margins depend on artificially maintaining analogue scarcity in an age of digital abundance, are doing their best not just to preserve copyright but to extend it. We're effectively facing what has been called a 'second enclosure movement', in which more and more of the cultural commons is being privatised.[87] We need to ask ourselves, for example, how stretching copyright from its original term of 14 years (in both Britain and the US) to 70 years past the death of the creator (as is now the case in many jurisdictions) corresponds to the original intention of encouraging creators to keep creating?

From the point of view of users, there are at least two different issues here. First, there are excerpts of media or cultural products found within, say, blog postings and YouTube home videos or remixes, some of which may be examples of perfectly legal 'fair use' or 'fair dealing' (though such laws vary between jurisdictions). Nevertheless, takedown notices issued or lawsuits brought in these cases can be time-consuming and expensive to fight. And if you lose, the damages may be exorbitant. It goes right to the top, too: in the 2008 US Presidential race, both John McCain and Barack Obama found their campaigns hampered by takedown notices relating to TV footage on YouTube. The result? On the one hand, a crushing of amateur and pro-am creativity and culture. On the other, a chilling of free speech and commentary. Either way, it's censorship through the law.

Second, there are clearly illegal activities such as p2p sharing of songs. Napster, Kazaa, Grokster, Pirate Bay: new filesharing services spring up as quickly as record companies can slap them down or pen them in. However, despite the music industry's multimillion dollar lawsuits against such services, not to mention against its own customers, there's little evidence that filesharing in aggregate is anything other than revenue-neutral: it may in fact serve to boost the popularity of music (and ultimately profits), while possibly leading to a redistribution of income from a small number of big stars to a bigger number of smaller stars.[88] What's clear is that copyright laws are more and more out of step with social norms, especially those of the younger generation. And criminalising a whole generation, suggests Lawrence Lessig, is highly dangerous: a rerun, effectively, of US Prohibition.[89] The kids have company, too: many artists acknowledge that free downloads have contributed to their success in a variety of ways.[90] The Arctic Monkeys famously launched themselves on the road to stardom by giving away their music for free at gigs and allowing fans to share it online, while long-established bands from the Nine Inch Nails to Radiohead are finding ways to sidestep musical middlemen. Trent Reznor, lead singer of the Nine Inch Nails, said in 2007 that it's time to '[e]liminate this dinosaur in the corner that's primarily taking all your money, based on a thieving business model, and [...] making enemies out of the people that [are] customers'. Record executives are 'in such a state of denial it's impossible for them to understand what's happening', he went on to explain in 2009: 'As an artist, *you* are now the marketer'.[91]

There are certainly other possible revenue models the music industry could explore – treating music as a service you tap into rather than a series of products you own; allowing filesharing and even remixing to boost popularity; or using recorded music as a loss leader to bump up concert attendance – but progress to date has been limited. These companies would do well to heed Jeff Jarvis's mixed metaphor warning: 'Beware the cash cow in the coal mine'.[92] In other words, don't let your current high profits blind you to the need to reinvent yourself to meet a changed future. Expensive analogue business models have limited prospects in a cheap digital culture.

As far back as 2003, DJ and singer Moby observed that: 'Record companies suing 12-year-old girls for file sharing is kind of like horse-and-buggy operators suing Henry Ford'.[93] For the moment, though, copyright law remains a battlefield on which yesterday's giants are fighting a rearguard action against today's artists and tomorrow's citizens to preserve yesterday's income. To the extent they succeed, it may be a Pyrrhic victory: they'll have removed their own products from circulation in the dominant remix culture which will increasingly route around established market players.[94] One thing is for sure: there'll be more skirmishes before the dust settles. In the meantime, states' willingness to support currently dominant market players by strengthening and policing copyright laws – artificially propping up the crumbling status quo and delaying real innovation – is a strategy of dubious long-term benefit, not just for individuals but for markets as a whole.

But there's another factor in the mix. Legal arguments may become moot as the online environment, where (computer) code is law, gradually turns into a space of 'perfect control'.[95] As noted in Chapter 2, we're seeing the growth of trusted computing and the proliferation of non-generative and tethered devices. We're also seeing the growth of digital rights management (DRM), as limitations are built into the code underpinning digital copies of cultural works. In short: you don't fully own what you've bought. Want to copy the song you've paid to download? You can't. Want to watch the film on a different device? You can't. Want to skip the ads? You can't. Code as law, which may entail regulation that goes far beyond everyday law, is self-enforcing.[96]

There's little question that similar levels of technical control will appeal to states. Why go through messy legal arguments when the architecture of the technology provides much better options for censorship? Non-generative and tethered technologies are much easier not just for companies but for governments to regulate. Cloud computing, where individuals no longer store their own data, facilitates surveillance. For terrorists and paedophiles, this isn't good news – but both have the means and the will to find ways around it. For anyone else who wants to use new technologies to write their own story, especially if they don't have the wherewithal to circumvent surveillance and censorship, it's very bad news indeed.

Future stories

The original purpose of the net 'was to connect anyone on the network to anyone else. It was up to the people connected to figure out why they wanted to be in touch in the first place'.[97] To a large extent the net still works that way. People connect to find friendship and love. People connect to find sexual partners. People connect to mash up cultural products. People connect to write citizen newspapers. People connect to blog against poverty. People connect to organise demonstrations. People connect to commit crimes or acts of terror. People connect to swap child porn.

There's no doubt that some of these connections demand state – and perhaps market – intervention. Most don't. But make no mistake: those who have a vested interest in controlling the net's free speech, from authoritarian regimes and nervous governments to media corporations and social conservatives, are playing on our fear of terrorism and our aversion for paedophilia to build a moral mandate for policing the net more tightly. It's been suggested that the 'global crew of Digital Natives is a far better bet than the dictators in the long run'[98] when it comes to battles over the freedom of the internet. But what if those who seek to restrict the net don't look like dictators? What if they come to us in the guise of paternalistic Western governments promising (ironically enough) to protect our political freedoms? What if they come to us as socially and morally concerned governments promising to protect our children? What if they come to us as music companies promising to protect our favourite artists?

Naturally, censorship and resistance tend to be mutually reinforcing. That's clear from the comments of those who've had to deal with the most repressive regimes: 'They block us and we evade the blocks. It goes on every day. They code, we decode', one Iranian blogger told *The Boston Globe*. 'If you're clever enough [online], you can find a way around government rules', says a Chinese book editor.[99] Most citizens of Western countries haven't needed to play by such codes, but already Australian IT experts have begun to promote details of tried-and-tested ways to bypass net filters. Just in case.

Yet it shouldn't be a case of choosing between states, markets and networks. We need all of them to keep checks on each other. Although many governments have colluded with the culture, entertainment and media industries over copyright law, they still play an important role in regulating markets. They need to step in where markets don't or won't: ensuring universal internet access and educational provision; outlawing child pornography; or challenging Western corporate complicity with authoritarian states. The last point highlights the fact that not all governments are alike and that greater protection of internet freedoms can be demanded by citizens of more liberal states. In that vein, companies like Google, Microsoft and Yahoo! have been summoned to US Congressional hearings, with the executives of Yahoo! being described as technological and financial 'giants' but moral 'pygmies' by late US Congressman Tom Lantos, referring to the company's role in Shi Tao's arrest.[100] Under political and public pressure, Yahoo! has since had a change of heart, reflected, notably, in its lobbying of the Bush administration in 2008 to press for the release of jailed Chinese dissidents.[101] Meanwhile, US politicians have drafted a Global Online Freedom Act, with some EU politicians keen on doing the same.[102]

Although technology corporations have colluded with authoritarian governments, and although culture, entertainment and media corporations have pushed many governments into extending copyright, markets have been an important ally of individual freedoms, given capitalism's disinterest in the voting patterns, religious affiliations or sexual proclivities of its consumers – well, at least as long as they keep consuming. Markets tend to view the 'imposition of national boundaries on the Internet [as] a barrier to progress', as stated in a recent OECD report,[103] and it was thanks to the commercial demand for safe online transactions that the US Government pulled back on plans to outlaw fully encrypted communications.[104] Of course, just as governments differ, so do companies: the interests of technology companies are sometimes at odds with those of culture, entertainment and media companies, with whom the former often refuse to play ball on censoring net users. Some technology companies support educational initiatives or online civic spaces and, for those which share the liberal web 2.0 ethos, there comes a point at which they refuse to collude with governments: Wikipedia and WordPress (the blog provider), for example, have allowed their pages to be blocked rather than censoring material for the Chinese market, while Google has refused to offer its email or blogging services there.[105] Notwithstanding its censoring of search results in China, for which it has been heavily criticised, Google has described censorship as its 'No. 1 barrier to trade'.[106] Recently, refusing to bow to South Korea's real-name registration law of April 2009, Google decided instead to block users from posting videos or comments to Korean YouTube, suggesting they do so through other countries'

YouTube sites.[107] There's also cause for hope in the 2008 signing of the Global Network Initiative, a voluntary agreement by Google, Microsoft, Yahoo! and other companies to abide by a common set of principles to 'resist[ ] efforts by governments that seek to enlist companies in acts of censorship and surveillance that violate international standards'.[108]

It would be naive to imagine networks can replace states or markets, but they can survive, even thrive, in the spaces between them, providing alternative modes of interaction and coordination, and allowing networked individuals to resist or circumvent some of the restrictions of states and markets. Networks can offer many individuals a voice – and those voices, collectively, are beginning to echo loudly in the halls of power and the marketplaces of the world. In years to come we can expect to hear a lot more from NGOs like the Electronic Frontier Foundation, Electronic Frontiers Australia, Electronic Frontier Canada, and the Open Rights Group (UK), which are native to the digitally networked medium whose freedoms they defend; we can expect to see more university-led initiatives like Herdict from the Berkman Center for Internet and Society at Harvard University, which is building collective intelligence about censorship through the efforts of a global network of concerned scholars and citizens; and we can expect to see rising numbers of pre-digital NGOs drawing new energy from the digital universe and its network-ready inhabitants.

We've seen again and again that technology has certain affordances but they don't necessarily determine how it's used. That's why we're witnessing intensifying competition over whose stories technology will support: those of liberal or authoritarian states? Those of technology companies or entertainment companies? Those of networked individuals? Or some combination of the above?

The role of education

While education has long been subject to the political dictates of individual states, and while it is increasingly influenced by market principles, university education in particular predates both modern states and modern economies. Despite political and market pressures, universities have retained much of their original character which, as Yochai Benkler notes, is based on a 'high intensity of communication within the academic community, among people engaged in the practice of conversation, writing, mutual commentary, and critique'.[109] Communication and collaboration are, by now, a familiar combination. So it's hardly surprising that, as Benkler observes, there's a heavy academic presence in many open source and open access projects, and that we've seen the rise of large-scale distributed research initiatives like the Human Genome Project. Universities, then, are well placed to offer an alternative organisational model to those of states and markets. As the locus of many teacher training programs, universities are also well placed to offer leadership to the whole education system. And the education system, whatever its shortcomings, is still the best opportunity most people have to access spaces where they can learn to think independently outside societal conventions.

It's important that teacher training programs show teachers how, from within the education system, they can introduce their students to – and model for them – the power of networks and networking technologies. Students should come to understand that political and social engagement no longer have to end at the ballot box, and that they can be much more than passive consumers of industrially produced cultural products. Clearly, their attention should also be drawn to the limitations and drawbacks of networks, as well as to the interactions of governments and corporations with the internet and networked individuals. They have to understand the nature of surveillance and censorship; they need to know when to be careful and why:

> Someday, sooner than you may like, big corporations and governments will know every copyrighted work you read, listen to, and watch. Anyone with a sense of history should fear such a system.[110]

But it's not just about fear. It's about having a context in which to make informed decisions as citizens and voters and, perhaps one day, as civil rights activists or human rights campaigners. That means, too, that students need to know what's happening not only in their own countries but in distant parts of the world.

For, as important as local and national stories may be, our students will also be global citizens who must deal with global issues as they write global narratives. Those who have a grasp of digital tools and digital networks, and an understanding of digital dangers, will have the best chance of ensuring that their voices, and those of their communities, are heard in the halls of power and the marketplaces of the world. They'll be able to ensure that the shaping of global narratives is not left solely to states and corporations – and indeed, they'll be able to help shape states and corporations from within.

6

Many *baas* & ^^^^^

An ecological lens

The Scottish schoolgirl we met at the start of this book complained of a holiday landscape populated only by *baas* & ^^^^. Yet we may actually need a greater focus on *baas* & ^^^^ to help us deal with contemporary technology. That may mean pausing to consider our physical and mental health, and perhaps taking tech-free breaks to recoup our shattered attention. It may mean stepping back to think about the effects of runaway technology on the natural ecosystems around us. And, in time, it may mean beginning to sketch out a holistic and sustainable planetary story.

Biology

Digital technologies have mixed effects on health. Their drawbacks range from broken attention and rising stress levels, as discussed in Chapter 4, to sleep deprivation for the teens who prefer surfing to sleeping or who leave their mobiles switched on all night.[1] At the extreme end of the scale, we hear tales of the deaths of Chinese and South Korean gamers who've collapsed after playing for days on end.[2] With their numerous treatment centres, China and South Korea are now leading the global battle against the spread of internet addiction.[3] While many psychologists agree that generalised net addiction exists as a condition in its own right, most advise that it's often about other addictions to, say, gambling or sex – which, however, the net facilitates.[4] Of course, many people turn to the net for help with their health problems, but for those who lack appropriate literacies or medical knowledge there are considerable dangers of misdiagnosis or even the development of 'cyberchondria'.[5] On the other hand, there's a growing store of vetted information thanks to initiatives such as Medpedia, and a complementary store of patient-generated reports on illnesses and treatments thanks to initiatives such as PatientsLikeMe. Some people may visit a health education island or medical clinic in Second Life; others are turning to blogging or social networking sites to help them deal with serious illness; and transplant donors have even been found through Facebook.[6] Meanwhile, brain imaging research indicates that web searches may be more effective than book reading in stimulating older brains.[7]

It is in fact the effect of digital technologies on the brain which, in the long term, may turn out to be most significant for human biology. It's long been known that learning causes physical changes in the brain, with repetition reinforcing certain circuits and the effects being strongest in young brains with their extra plasticity.[8] There are gains: young people, it seems, may be better adapted than their older peers to operating in fast-moving, digitally driven environments, with greater skills in filtering information, making quick decisions, and even multitasking, and perhaps greater creativity as well.[9] But there are losses too: the ability to focus carefully or think deeply (perhaps reflected in the rise of disorders like attention deficit disorder [ADD], attention deficit hyperactivity disorder [ADHD], and adult ADHD), as well as the ability to express and read emotions (possibly reflected in a rise in autism).[10] Neuroscientist Gary Small makes this recommendation:

> [Y]ou can take steps to address this [lack of balance]. It means taking time to cut back on technology, like having a family dinner, to find a balance. It is important to understand how technology is affecting our lives and our brains and take control of it.[11]

Like the technology experts mentioned in Chapter 4, Small doesn't suggest abandoning technology but approaching it in a balanced way. In short: if txtspk has its place in our world, so too do *baas & ^^^^^*.

Today's biological balancing act may soon get much harder. The convergence of information technology, biotechnology and nanotechnology, observes neuroscientist Susan Greenfield, heralds a future where barriers will collapse completely between the virtual and the real, the old and the young, and the self and the world.[12] We are, in fact, about to enter the scifi-like era of cyborgs where the machine is integrated with the human and we finally escape the biological limits of the brain. At one end of the spectrum, neurochips may help us manipulate computers and write mentally – just by thinking, without the need to touch a keypad or a mouse.[13] Maybe we'll also find our mental processing power routinely enhanced by technology. Google co-founder Larry Page puts it simply: 'you can imagine your brain being augmented by Google'. Google's other co-founder, Sergey Brin, asks: 'Why not improve the brain? Perhaps in the future, we can attach a little version of Google that you just plug into your brain'.[14] At the far end of the spectrum, futurists like Vernor Vinge and Ray Kurzweil breathlessly anticipate what's sometimes called the 'technological singularity'; that is, the point at which artificial intelligence (AI) will surpass human cognitive abilities and go on to create ever greater intelligences.[15] And after that? Well, assuming the AI is well-disposed towards humans, we're told, we may eventually find our minds uploaded into machines – leading, effectively, to immortality.

Sceptics point out that, some 400 years after Descartes, many technologists are still prey to the illusion that the mind can be separated from the body and that intelligence can be reduced to abstract patterns of information.[16] Indeed, as Nick Carr suggests, there's a disturbing kind of

"There was no umbilical cord. These days, babies are connected by Bluetooth."

Figure 6.1. Biology meets technology. Cartoon © Randy Glasbergen, 2008, <www.glasbergen.com>.

misanthropy behind plans to merge the mind and the machine, sloughing off the body in the process.[17] In the meantime (and, dare I suggest, for a long time to come) the fallacy of neglecting the body, and its corollary, neglecting the environment that sustains the body, are probably the greatest dangers we face. Technology which ignores biology and ecology has no future.

Ecology

Digital technologies are energy-hungry. ICTs are currently responsible for around 2 per cent of the world's total carbon dioxide emissions, about the same as aviation,[18] while the internet's energy demands are growing by around 10 per cent a year.[19] Newly emerging figures should give us pause for thought: a Google search may produce between 0.2g and 10g of carbon, depending on its length and the equipment used.[20] The power eaten up by spam in 2008 could have run 2.4 million US homes.[21] A Second Life avatar, it's been speculated, may consume as much energy as an average Brazilian.[22] Meanwhile there's an ecological tragedy emerging at the limit of the digital divide, thanks to the dumping of Western e-waste in countries like China, Ghana and Nigeria, where the locals – many of them kids – rake through toxic materials or, worse still, release toxic chemicals as they burn old computer parts to retrieve precious metals.[23]

There's some cause for cautious environmental optimism. It's partly due to technological trends: we're already seeing a decline in office paper use[24] and, thanks to cloud computing, we may soon see a decline in underused machines. It's partly due to markets, with major companies like Apple, IBM and Microsoft implementing environmental strategies, and Google investing in alternative energies – having recently been granted a patent on wave-powered floating data centres.[25] It's partly due to governments intervening in markets with legislation like the EU's Waste Electrical and Electronic Equipment (WEEE) Directive or the Australian Government's plan to regulate the energy efficiency of technology.[26] It's partly due to NGOs like the UK-based Computer Aid International and ReCOM. It's partly due to grassroots networking through initiatives like Freecycle on Yahoo! Groups or the EcoCommons sim launched in Second Life in 2009. In short, we've made a start. 'Green IT' is finding its way onto corporate, governmental and public agendas. Importantly, we see how states, markets, NGOs and networks can complement each other as we address common problems. But as the still growing mounds of e-waste in West Africa and East Asia demonstrate all too clearly, our shared ecological battles are far from over. We need to do more. And quickly.

God as a wiki

There is now a GodTube.com (or at least there was, until it was renamed tangle.com in 2009). There's an automated service, You've Been Left Behind, designed to email non-Christians six days after the Rapture. Even the Pope demonstrated his tech credentials by texting at World Youth Day in Sydney in 2008. But, although Christianity is well-represented on the web along with all the major faiths and a host of minor ones, internet age spirituality is about much more than new channels for conventional religious expression. For thousands of years, Western culture has linked spirituality to *immateriality*.[27] Religion, like technology, is about transcending our physical limitations, escaping the body, leaving it behind. Early commentators immediately perceived a spiritual aspect in the immateriality of cyberspace, with Michael Benedikt describing it in 1991 as a 'Heavenly City' and Nicole Stenger exclaiming: 'We will all become angels, and for eternity!'[28] Perhaps that's what's made it so easy – too easy, even – to displace our quest for salvation onto the internet, this arena of digital profiles, electronic avatars and virtual worlds.[29] Perhaps that helps explain the drive to upload our minds in a technological singularity that will allow us to live forever.

Of course, we shouldn't be surprised at the linking of technology and spirituality if we recall the roots of our contemporary digital tools in the 1960s, an era which loosely mixed 'social and personal transcendence',[30] LSD and spirituality. It's not only about immateriality, though. It's also about *connectedness*. As one writer commented about the members of the Electronic Frontier Foundation: 'Older and wiser now, they're on the road again, without the bus and the acid, but dispensing many similar-sounding bromides: Turn on, jack in, get connected'.[31] Theologians and religious leaders, too, have been struck by the sense of connectedness which has resonated so strongly with hippies and geeks. The work of Christian theologian Jennifer Cobb suggests that the internet has 'merely hardwired our preexisting interconnectedness' and 'externally actualized our evolving psycho-spiritual ties with one other'.[32] For Rabbi Joshua Hammerman, humanity is moving away from the old 'Shepherd' metaphor of a God who takes responsibility for humans and towards a new vision of a God existing, as in the tradition of Martin Buber, between humans: 'The prevailing metaphor of this new cybervillage we are creating, *the Web*, is how I think we all are beginning to think of God'. In essence, he suggests: '*We find God on the Internet because it binds us all as One*'.[33] Of course, the degree of connectedness has only grown with the advent of web 2.0, as clearly shown in Matthew Hurst's map of connections in the blogosphere (Figure 6.2). But perhaps the ultimate web 2.0 tool is the wiki. Cass Sunstein, as we've seen, has speculated on whether human knowledge can be seen as a wiki. Is it perhaps conceivable, in homage to Jesuit priest Pierre Teilhard de Chardin's notion of a 'noösphere', and in the tradition of process theology, to view God as a wiki, a global collective consciousness, binding us all and in a continual process of becoming?

Yet, in a reflection of the global mood, international conversation has begun to shift away from this kind of focus on the internet and spirituality, prevalent around the turn of the millennium, and towards a focus on ecology. Actually, there are clear parallels between our spiritual and ecological discussions, both predicated on global connectedness and a common purpose. But there's a retreat from immateriality in the crucial recognition that the physical world matters after all: the oceans and the skies, the trees and the animals, and our own bodies and brains. If we poison the world and ourselves, the internet, with all its wonders and perils, ceases to matter. Yet perhaps the internet holds part of the answer, pointing us towards a solution, the only kind of solution, in fact, that will be workable: a collective, collaborative one. Indeed, because of its sensitivity to patterns of change among those it connects, researchers at Stockholm University have recently proposed that the net could be used as an environmental early warning system.[34] Technology entrepreneur Elon Musk has suggested that

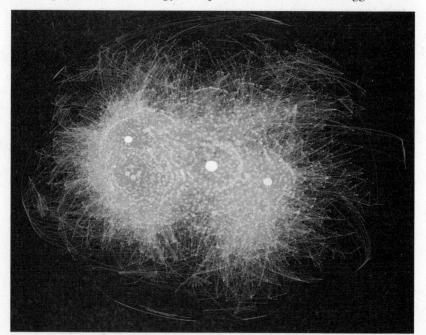

Figure 6.2. The connectedness of the net. Image: Internet Blog Map. © Matthew Hurst/Science Photo Library.

the arrival of the net 'was like humanity getting a nervous system. It's as if each of the cells in the human organism had access to all the information, the cumulative information, of humanity'.[35] Similarly, the Head of the Global Viral Forecasting Initiative, Nathan Wolfe, has observed that '[i]f the internet is humanity's planetary nervous system, we are now building our planetary immune system'.[36] It's the connectedness, in the end, that counts. It's all one ecosystem. As David Levy says: 'our true nature can only be found in our relatedness; in our very being we are inseparable from one another, nature, the universe'.[37] Call it spirituality, call it ecology, or just call it networking. It may be our only path to a sustainable future.

A world of diversity

Yes, digital technologies contribute in their own way to biological and ecological damage, and to political and social discord. But they may also represent our best hope for addressing planetary issues. That is, if we're willing to combat phenomena that make the net divisive rather than connective: the digital divide and cultural imperialism. If we're willing to protest against those who want to control its political and civic freedoms: (some) states and (some) corporations. If we're willing to stand up to those who want to limit its personal and social choices to the ones they've made in their own (mostly offline) lives: the purveyors of moral panics and national net filters. If we're willing to ignore those who'd like to restrict technology to serving up mono-literate texts and pre-digital drills: literacy conservatives and back-to-basics campaigners.

Just as a healthy ecosystem depends on biodiversity, collective intelligence relies on human diversity. But we need a way to connect that diversity, to direct it into collaborative channels. Right now, with a planet in ecological, political and social crisis, we need connective channels and collaborative platforms more than ever, and we need the collective intelligence they can facilitate. In short, we need a way to build a global story, one that's peaceful, equitable and environmentally sustainable, out of a host of national, local and individual stories. Digital technologies like the net, the web, and especially web 2.0, with its liberalising, democratising, connective ethos, give us a starting point. They could serve us well if we choose to work with rather than against their affordances. And the place to begin exploring and exploiting them? It's got to be education.

NOTES

NB: Unless otherwise stated, urls were last visited on 31 May 2009.

1 – Many lenses: An introduction

1   Cited in J. Johnston, 'Teachers call for urgent action as pupils write essays in text-speak', *Sunday Herald*, 2 Mar. 2003, p. 4. Apart from the removal of paragraphing, the text included here follows that cited by Johnston. Note, however, that many of the versions available on the net contain slight variations. For discussions of the implications of this now famous story about txtspk, see: L. Beason, *Eyes Before Ease: The Unsolved Mysteries and Secret Histories of Spelling*, McGraw-Hill, New York, 2006, p. 35; G. Goggin, *Cell Phone Culture: Mobile Technology in Everyday Life*, Routledge, London, 2006, pp. 115–16; I. Snyder, *The Literacy Wars: Why Teaching Children to Read and Write is a Battleground in Australia*, Allen & Unwin, Crows Nest, NSW, 2008, p. 179. The authenticity of the text is questioned in D. Crystal, *Txtng: The Gr8 Db8*, Oxford University Press, Oxford, 2008, pp. 24–5, 151–2. Its severely abbreviated form suggests it is not a naturally occurring example of txtspk and has been purposely constructed to be impenetrable, although that doesn't mean a Scottish schoolgirl couldn't have been responsible for it.

2   M. Prensky, 'Digital natives, digital immigrants', *On the Horizon*, vol. 9, no. 5, Oct. 2001, <www.marcprensky.com/writing/Prensky %20–%20Digital%20Natives,%20Digital%20 Immigrants%20–%20Part1.pdf>; M. Prensky, 'Digital natives, digital immigrants, Part II: Do they really *think* differently?', *On the Horizon*, vol. 9, no. 6, Dec. 2001, <www. marcprensky.com/writing/Prensky%20–%20Digital%20Natives,%20Digital%20 Immigrants%20–%20Part2.pdf>.

3   D. Tapscott, *Growing Up Digital: The Rise of the Net Generation*, McGraw-Hill, New York, 1998; D. Tapscott, *Grown Up Digital: How the Net Generation is Changing Your World*, McGraw-Hill, New York, 2009.

4   The remainder of the text reads: 'But my parents were so worried because of 9/11 that they decided to stay in Scotland and spend two weeks up north. Up north, what

110

you see is what you get – nothing. I was very, very, very bored in the middle of nowhere. Nothing but sheep and mountains. At any rate, my parents were happy – they said it could be worse, and that they were happy for the peace and quiet…I don't think so! I wanted to go home as soon as possible, to see my mates again. Today, I came back to school. I feel very angelic because I have done all my homework. Now it's business as usual …'

5   Judith Gillespie cited in Johnston, 'Teachers call for urgent action'.

6   'Is txt mightier than the word?', *BBC News*, 4 Mar. 2003, <news.bbc.co.uk/2/hi/uk_news/2814235.stm>.

7   H. Norbrook, 'If they won't write, get them to text', *The Guardian Weekly*, 15 May 2003, <education.guardian.co.uk/tefl/story/0,5500,956003,00.html>.

8   'Is txt mightier than the word?'

9   J. Clarkson, 'Proper writing is like so overr8ted, innit kids', *The Sunday Times*, 29 Aug. 2004, p. 17. Clarkson doesn't specifically mention the essay by the Scottish schoolgirl, but his article touches on the broader debate over txtspk in the British press.

10   'Wots rude', *Insight*, SBS TV [Aus.], 11 Mar. 2008, <news.sbs.com.au/insight/episode/index/id/32>.

11   G. Motteram and S. Ioannou-Georgiou, 'Are teachers fit for web 6.0?', paper presented at New and Emerging Technologies in ELT [English Language Teaching], Loyola College, Chennai, India, 3–5 Aug. 2007.

12   S. Moulthrop, 'No more literacies!', paper presented at Computers and Writing Conference, University of Baltimore, 11 Jun. 2004, <iat.ubalt.edu/moulthrop/talks/cw04/>.

13   T. Brabazon, *Digital Hemlock: Internet Education and the Poisoning of Teaching*, University of New South Wales Press, Sydney, 2002, p. 152.

14   danah boyd cited in K. Poulsen, 'Scenes from the MySpace backlash', *Wired*, 27 Feb. 2006, <www.wired.com/politics/law/news/2006/02/70254>.

15   The term 'context collision' is drawn from the work of danah boyd. See for example, d. boyd, 'Friends, Friendsters, and Top 8: Writing community into being on social network sites', *First Monday*, vol. 11, no. 12, 4 Dec. 2006, <firstmonday.org/htbin/cgiwrap/bin/ojs/index.php/fm/article/view/1418/1336>.

16   The term 'continuous partial attention' was coined by Linda Stone. See for example, L. Stone, 'Fine dining with mobile devices', *The Huffington Post*, 9 Jan. 2008, <www.huffingtonpost.com/linda-stone/fine-dining-with-mobile-d_b_80819.html>.

17   M. Prensky, 'Engage me or enrage me', paper presented to the Department of Education and Training, Perth, Western Australia, 31 May 2007.

18   J. Schultz, '2020 unleashed – Open government', *ABC* [Aus.], 21 Apr. 2008, <www.abc.net.au/unleashed/stories/s2222596.htm>.

19   'The political potential of new media', *The Economist*, 17 Apr. 2008, <www.economist.com/world/britain/displaystory.cfm?story_id=11053170>.

20   H. Rheingold, *Smart Mobs: The Next Social Revolution*, Basic Books, Cambridge, MA, 2002.

21   A. Giddens, *Modernity and Self-Identity: Self and Society in the Late Modern Age*, Polity, Cambridge, 1991.

2 – Many clouds: A technological lens

1   F. Turner, *From Counterculture to Cyberculture: Stewart Brand, the Whole Earth Network, and the Rise of Digital Utopianism*, University of Chicago Press, Chicago, 2006, p. 2.

2   J. Goldsmith and T. Wu, *Who Controls the Internet? Illusions of a Borderless World*, Oxford University Press, New York, 2006, pp. 22–7; J. Harkin, *Cyburbia: The Dangerous Idea That's Changing How We Live and Who We Are*, Little, Brown, London, 2009, esp. pp. 32–93; J. Markoff, *What the Dormouse Said: How the Sixties Counterculture Shaped the Personal Computer Industry*, Viking, New York, 2005; Turner, *From Counterculture to Cyberculture*.

3   S. Levy, *Insanely Great: The Life and Times of Macintosh, the Computer that Changed Everything*, Viking, New York, 1994, p. 42.

4   S. Brand, 'We owe it all to the hippies', *Time*, 1 Mar. 1995, <www.time.com/time/ magazine/article/0,9171,982602,00.html>.

5   S. Jobs, '"You've got to find what you love," Jobs says', *Stanford Report*, 14 Jun. 2005, <news-service.stanford.edu/news/2005/june15/jobs-061505.html>.

6   Turner, *From Counterculture to Cyberculture*.

7   D. D. Clark, 'A cloudy crystal ball: Visions of the future', paper presented at the 24th Internet Engineering Task Force, MIT, Cambridge, MA, 13–17 Jul. 1992, <xys.ccert.edu.cn/ reference/future_ietf_92.pdf>.

8   Jane Metcalfe cited in Turner, *From Counterculture to Cyberculture*, p. 208.

9   *Time*, 25 Dec. 2006–1 Jan. 2007, <www.time.com/time/covers/0,16641,20061225,00.html>.

10   C. Leadbeater (and 257 other people), *We-Think*, Profile Books, London, 2008, p. 27.

11   Social networking, for example, took off in large part thanks to the gay New York men and the attendees of the annual Burning Man festival who made early use of Friendster; see d. boyd, 'None of this is real: Identity and participation in Friendster', in J. Karaganis (ed.), *Structures of Participation in Digital Culture*, Social Science Research Council, New York, 2007, esp. pp. 136–40, <www.ssrc.org/blogs/books/wp-content/ uploads/2008/02/8-boyd.pdf>. While many virtual worlds, including today's field leader, Second Life, are not actually web-based, they are often associated with the ethos of web 2.0. Creator Philip Rosedale has linked his inspiration for Second Life to Burning Man; see W. J. Au, *The Making of Second Life: Notes from the New World*, Collins, New York, 2008, pp. 20–1, 31. Linden Lab, the company behind Second Life, sponsors an annual virtual Burning Man tribute called 'Burning Life'; see M. Rymaszewski, W. J. Au and M. Wallace, *Second Life: The Official Guide*, John Wiley, San Francisco, 2007, pp. 293–4.

12   T. O'Reilly, 'What is web 2.0: Design patterns and business models for the next generation of software', *O'Reilly*, 30 Sep. 2005, p. 1, <www.oreillynet.com/pub/a/ oreilly/tim/news/2005/09/30/what-is-web-20.html>.

13   ibid., p. 4.

14   ibid., p. 3.

15   J. Rosen, 'The people formerly known as the audience', *PressThink*, 27 Jun. 2006, <journalism.nyu.edu/pubzone/weblogs/pressthink/2006/06/27/ppl_frmr.html>.

16   C. Lankshear and M. Knobel, *New Literacies: Everyday Practices and Classroom Learning*, 2nd edn., Open University Press, Maidenhead, Berkshire, 2006, p. 49.

17   The Association of Virtual Worlds, *The Blue Book: A Consumer Guide to Virtual Worlds*, iVinnie, 2009, <www.associationofvirtualworlds.com/thebluebook/the_blue_book_ january_2009_5th_edition.pdf>.

18   J. Zittrain, *The Future of the Internet and How to Stop It*, Allen Lane, London, 2008, pp. 34, 80–94, <futureoftheinternet.org/download>.

19   Australian Communications and Media Authority, *Top Six Trends in Communications and Media Technologies, Applications and Services—Possible Implications*, Canberra, 2008, <www.acma.gov.au/webwr/_assets/main/lib310658/top_six_trends.pdf>.

20   O'Reilly, 'What is web 2.0', p. 4.

21   Zittrain, *The Future of the Internet*, p. 70.

22   Zittrain, *The Future of the Internet*. See also: H. Abelson, K. Ledeen and H. Lewis, *Blown to Bits: Your Life, Liberty, and Happiness After the Digital Explosion*, Addison-Wesley, Upper Saddle River, NJ, 2008.

23   J. Zittrain, 'Do we need a new internet?', *The Future of the Internet* [blog], 17 Feb. 2009, <futureoftheinternet.org/do-we-need-a-new-internet>.

24   N. Carr, *The Big Switch: Rewiring the World, From Edison to Google*, W. W. Norton, New York, 2008, p. 12.

25   J. Belluz, 'Pups on parade as police turn to Facebook', *The Times*, 16 Oct. 2008, <technology.timesonline.co.uk/tol/news/tech_and_web/article4958179.ece>; 'Facebook aiding search for missing Aussie', *ABC News* [Aus.], 27 Sep. 2008, <www.abc.net.au/ news/stories/2008/09/27/2375955.htm>; M. Taylor, 'MI6 seeks recruits on Facebook',

The Guardian, 29 Sep. 2008, <www.guardian.co.uk/technology/2008/sep/29/facebook.workandcareers>; A. Caldwell, 'Facebook features as long arm of the law', *The World Today*, ABC Radio [Aus.], 16 Dec. 2008, <www.abc.net.au/worldtoday/content/2008/s2447627.htm>.

26   J. Boorstin, 'Virtual meetings get a 2nd life', *CNBC*, 27 Feb. 2009, <www.cnbc.com/id/29429445>; A. Semuels, 'Corporate America's Second Life', *Los Angeles Times*, 10 May 2008, <articles.latimes.com/2008/may/10/business/fi-secondlife10>.

27   N. Abrahams, 'Virtual crime is on the rise', *The Sydney Morning Herald*, 3 Nov. 2008, <www.smh.com.au/news/technology/biztech/virtual-crime-is-on-the-rise/2008/11/03/1225560726242.html>; 'Dutch court finds youths guilty of "virtual theft"', *The Daily Telegraph*, 22 Oct. 2008, <www.telegraph.co.uk/scienceandtechnology/3358885/Dutch-court-finds-youths-guilty-of-virtual-theft.html>.

28   R. Edwards, 'Woman divorces husband for having a "virtual" affair on Second Life', *The Daily Telegraph*, 15 Nov. 2008, <www.telegraph.co.uk/scienceandtechnology/technology/3453273/Woman-divorces-husband-for-having-a-virtual-affair-on-Second-Life.html>; Abrahams, 'Virtual crime is on the rise'; R. L. Parry, 'Jilted Japanese woman questioned by police after "murdering" her virtual husband', *The Times*, 25 Oct. 2008, <www.timesonline.co.uk/tol/news/world/asia/article5008156.ece>.

29   Commission of the European Communities, *Future Networks and the Internet: Early Challenges Regarding the 'Internet of Things'*, Commission Staff Working Document, Brussels, 29 Sep. 2008, <ec.europa.eu/information_society/eeurope/i2010/docs/future_internet/swp_internet_things.pdf>.

30   J. Battelle, *The Search: How Google and Its Rivals Rewrote the Rules of Business and Transformed Our Culture*, Portfolio, New York, 2005, p. 254.

31   Commission of the European Communities, *Future Networks and the Internet*, p. 8.

32   D. Buckingham (with reference to Raymond Williams), 'Introducing identity', in D. Buckingham (ed.), *Youth, Identity, and Digital Media*, MIT Press, Cambridge, MA, 2008, p. 12, <www.mitpressjournals.org/doi/pdf/10.1162/dmal.9780262524834.001>.

33   C. Shirky, *Here Comes Everybody: The Power of Organizing Without Organizations*, Allen Lane, New York, 2008, p. 105.

34   S. Bax, 'CALL—Past, present and future', *System*, vol. 31, 2003, pp. 13–28. See also: A. Chambers and S. Bax, 'Making CALL work: Towards normalisation', *System*, vol. 34, 2006, pp. 465–79; S. Bax, *Computers and Technology in Language Education: Past, Present and Future* (in preparation).

35   d. boyd, 'The Economist debate on social "networking"', *Zephoria*, 15 Jan. 2008, <www.zephoria.org/thoughts/archives/2008/01/15/the_economist_d.html>.

36   See the thought-provoking discussion of emergent and established CALL in M. Levy and G. Stockwell, *CALL Dimensions: Options and Issues in Computer-Assisted Language Learning*, Lawrence Erlbaum, Mahwah, NJ, 2006, pp. 239–53.

37   A. Feenberg, *Critical Theory of Technology*, Oxford University Press, Oxford, 1991, p. 14.

3 – Many literacies: A pedagogical lens

1   Leadbeater, *We-Think*, p. 147; Tapscott, *Grown Up Digital*, p. 122.

2   M. Warschauer, 'The paradoxical future of digital learning', *Learning Inquiry*, vol. 1, p. 42.

3   G. Sinclair, M. McClaren and M. J. Griffin, *E-learning and Beyond: A Discussion Paper Prepared as Part of the Campus 2020 Process for the British Columbia Ministry of Advanced Education*, 2006, p. 23, <www.aved.gov.bc.ca/campus2020/documents/e-learning.pdf>.

4   L. Johnson, A. Levine and R. Smith, *The Horizon Report: 2008 Australia–New Zealand Edition*, The New Media Consortium, Austin, TX, 2008, p. 2, <www.nmc.org/pdf/2008-Horizon-Report-ANZ.pdf>.

5   CISCO, *Equipping Every Learner for the 21st Century*, CISCO Systems, 2008, p. 11, <www.cisco.com/web/about/citizenship/socio-economic/docs/GlobalEdWP.pdf>.

6   G. Healy, 'Business wants graduates who can cope', *The Australian*, 18 Mar. 2009,

<www.theaustralian.news.com.au/story/0,25197,25201576-12332,00.html>.

7   See for example, C. Beck and C. Kosnik, *Innovations in Teacher Education: A Social Constructivist Approach*, SUNY Press, Albany, NY, 2006; B. Dalgarno, 'Interpretations of constructivism and consequences for computer assisted learning', *British Journal of Educational Technology*, vol. 32, no. 2, 2001, pp. 183–94; G. Finger, G. Russell, R. Jamieson-Proctor and N. Russell, *Transforming Learning with ICT: Making It Happen*, Pearson, Frenchs Forest, NSW, 2007, p. 119; D. H. Jonassen, 'Evaluating constructivistic learning', in T. M. Duffy and D. H. Jonassen (eds), *Constructivism and the Technology of Instruction: A Conversation*, Lawrence Erlbaum, Hillsdale, NJ, 1992, pp. 137–48.

8   T. Freedman, 'Introduction', in T. Freedman (ed.), *Coming of Age: An Introduction to the New World Wide Web*, Terry Freedman, Ilford, UK, 2006, p. 13, <fullmeasure.co.uk/Coming_of_age_v1-2.pdf>.

9   J. Palfrey and U. Gasser, *Born Digital: Understanding the First Generation of Digital Natives*, Basic Books, New York, 2008, p. 125.

10   A. Patty, 'Phone a friend in exams', *The Sydney Morning Herald*, 20 Aug. 2008, <www.smh.com.au/news/athome/phone-a-friend-in-exams/2008/08/20/1218911794460.html>.

11   D. Weinberger, *Everything is Miscellaneous: The Power of the New Digital Disorder*, Times Books, New York, 2007, p. 147.

12   J. Surowiecki, *The Wisdom of Crowds: Why the Many are Smarter than the Few*, Abacus, London, 2005.

13   J. Howe, *Crowdsourcing: Why the Power of the Crowd is Driving the Future of Business*, Crown Business, New York, 2008, pp. 233–7.

14   B. Alexander, 'Web 2.0: A new wave of innovation for teaching and learning?', *EDUCAUSE Review*, vol. 41, no. 2, Mar./Apr. 2006, p. 36, <net.educause.edu/ir/library/pdf/ERM0621.pdf>.

15   H. Jenkins, *Convergence Culture: Where Old and New Media Collide*, New edn., New York University Press, New York, 2008; H. Jenkins, K. Clinton, R. Purushotma, A. J. Robison and M. Weigel, *Confronting the Challenges of Participatory Culture: Media Education for the 21st Century*, The MacArthur Foundation, Chicago, 2006, <www.digitallearning.macfound.org/atf/cf/%7B7E45C7E0-A3E0-4B89-AC9C-E807E1B0AE4E%7D/JENKINS_WHITE_PAPER.PDF>. See also: H. Jenkins, 'Collective intelligence vs. the wisdom of crowds', *Confessions of an Aca-Fan*, 27 Nov. 2006, <www.henryjenkins.org/2006/11/collective_intelligence_vs_the.html>.

16   J. Giles, 'Internet encyclopaedias go head to head', *Nature*, no. 438, 15 Dec. 2005, pp. 900–1.

17   Jenkins, *Convergence Culture*, pp. 1–2.

18   Howe, *Crowdsourcing*, pp. 177–9. See also: Y. Benkler, *The Wealth of Networks: How Social Production Transforms Markets and Freedom*, Yale University Press, New Haven, CT, 2006, pp. 295–300; Leadbeater, *We-Think*, pp. 56–9.

19   A. Bruns, *Blogs, Wikipedia, Second Life, and Beyond: From Production to Produsage*, Peter Lang, New York, 2008, pp. 9–36.

20   C. Leadbeater and P. Miller, *The Pro-Am Revolution: How Enthusiasts are Changing Our Economy and Society*, Demos, London, 2004, blurb.

21   A. Lenhart and M. Madden, *Teen Content Creators and Consumers*, Pew Internet & American Life Project, Washington, 2 Nov. 2005, p. i, <www.pewinternet.org/PPF/r/166/report_display.aspx> (reporting on a survey conducted in late 2004); A. Lenhart, M. Madden, A. Rankin Macgill and A. Smith, *Teens and Social Media*, Pew Internet & American Life Project, Washington, 19 Dec. 2007, p. i, <www.pewinternet.org/Reports/2007/Teens-and-Social-Media.aspx> (reporting on a survey conducted in late 2006).

22   A. Bruns, *Gatewatching: Collaborative Online News Production*, Peter Lang, New York, 2005, p. 238.

23   W. W. Fisher, 'Theories of intellectual property', in S. R. Munzer (ed.), *New Essays in the Legal and Political Theory of Property*, Cambridge University Press, Cambridge, 2001, also available at: <cyber.law.harvard.edu/people/tfisher/iptheory.pdf>.

24   Jenkins et al., *Confronting the Challenges of Participatory Culture*, p. 10.

25   Bruns, *Blogs, Wikipedia, Second Life, and Beyond*, pp. 189–90.

26   Leadbeater, *We-Think*, p. xiii. Leadbeater states the authorship of his book as 'Charles Leadbeater (and 257 other people)'. For examples of writers' blogs, wikis and other websites which invite collaboration and commentary, see: Chris Anderson's *The Long Tail*, <www.longtail.com/the_long_tail/>; Charles Leadbeater's *We-Think*, <www.wethinkthebook.net/home.aspx>; Lawrence Lessig's *Anti-Lessig Reader*, <wiki.lessig.org/index.php/Anti-Lessig_Reader>; Don Tapscott and Anthony Williams' *Wikinomics*, <www.socialtext.net/wikinomics/index.cgi>; or McKenzie Wark's *Gamer Theory Version 2.0*, <www.futureofthebook.org/gamertheory2.0/>. Note that many of these are subject to change as the authors work on new projects.

27   Bruns, *Blogs, Wikipedia, Second Life, and Beyond*, p. 22.

28   C. Doctorow, *Content: Selected Essays on Technology, Creativity, Copyright, and the Future of the Future*, Tachyon, San Francisco, 2008, pp. 169–70.

29   C. R. Sunstein, *Infotopia: How Many Minds Produce Knowledge*, Oxford University Press, New York, 2006, pp. 9, 217.

30   See for example, B. Lane, 'Macquarie University opens up access to its academics' research papers', *The Australian*, 29 Aug. 2008, <www.theaustralian.news.com.au/story/0,25197,24260992-12332,00.html>; R. Mitchell, 'Harvard to collect, disseminate scholarly articles for faculty', *Harvard University Gazette*, 13 Feb. 2008, <www.news.harvard.edu/gazette/2008/02.14/99-fasvote.html>.

31   D. Gillmor, *We the Media: Grassroots Journalism By the People, For the People*, O'Reilly, Sebastopol, CA, 2006, p. xiv.

32   Lynne Brindley cited in Leadbeater, *We-Think*, pp. 144–5.

33   G. Hamel, 'The Facebook generation vs. the Fortune 500', *Gary Hamel's Management 2.0*, Wall Street Journal Blogs, 24 Mar. 2009, <blogs.wsj.com/management/2009/03/24/the-facebook-generation-vs-the-fortune-500/>.

34   Steven Johnson cited in Lankshear and Knobel, *New Literacies*, p. 250.

35   Eric Schmidt cited in T. L. Friedman, *The World is Flat: A Brief History of the Twenty-first Century*, New edn., Picador, New York, 2007, p. 183.

36   A. Wright, *Glut: Mastering Information through the Ages*, Joseph Henry Press, Washington, 2007, p. 204.

37   C. Doctorow, 'On "Digital Maoism: The Hazards of the New Online Collectivism" by Jaron Lanier', *Edge: The Reality Club*, 2006, <www.edge.org/discourse/digital_maoism.html>.

38   Stephen Colbert cited in M. Hesse, 'Truth: Can you handle it?', *The Washington Post*, 27 Apr. 2008, p. M01, <www.washingtonpost.com/wp-dyn/content/article/2008/04/25/AR2008042500922.html>.

39   See for example, A. Keen, *The Cult of the Amateur: How Today's Internet is Killing Our Culture and Assaulting Our Economy*, Nicholas Brealey, London, 2007; D. G. Wallace, *One Nation Under Blog: Forget the Facts…Believe What I Say!*, Brown Books, Dallas, 2008.

40   'Britannica's new site: More participation, collaboration from experts and readers', *Encyclopaedia Britannica Blog*, 3 Jun. 2008, <www.britannica.com/blogs/2008/06/britannicas-new-site-more-participation-collaboration-from-experts-and-readers/>; C. Sweeney, 'Britannica 2.0 shows Wikipedia how it's done', *The Times*, 22 Jan. 2009, <technology.timesonline.co.uk/tol/news/tech_and_web/article5564836.ece>.

41   A. Lih, *The Wikipedia Revolution: How a Bunch of Nobodies Created the World's Greatest Encyclopedia*, Aurum, London, 2009, esp. pp. 191–4, 221, 225–35.

42   M. Harvey, 'Wikipedia founder Jimmy Wales calls for pre-approval of changes', *The Times*, 26 Jan. 2009, <technology.timesonline.co.uk/tol/news/tech_and_web/the_web/article5593986.ece>.

43   Shirky, *Here Comes Everybody*, p. 139.

44   J. Wales, 'Challenging how knowledge is created', paper presented to Education.au, Melbourne, 27 Apr. 2007, MP3 (9), <www.educationau.edu.au/jahia/Jahia/home/cache/offonce/pid/605>.

45   Lih, *The Wikipedia Revolution*, p. 130.

46   See for example, D. Barton and M. Hamilton, 'Literacy practices', in D. Barton, M. Hamilton and R. Ivanič (eds), *Situated Literacies: Reading and Writing in Context*, Routledge, London, 2000, pp. 7–15; The New London Group, 'A pedagogy of multiliteracies: Designing social futures', in B. Cope and M. Kalantzis (eds), *Multiliteracies: Literacy Learning and the Design of Social Futures*, Routledge, London, 2000, pp. 9–37.

47   G. Kress, 'Visual and verbal modes of representation in electronically mediated communication: The potentials of new forms of text', in I. Snyder (ed.), *Page to Screen: Taking Literacy into the Electronic Era*, Allen & Unwin, St. Leonards, NSW, 1997, pp. 53–79.

48   D. Perkel (with reference to Andrea diSessa), 'Copy and paste literacy? Literacy practices in the production of a MySpace profile', in K. Drotner, H. Siggaard Jensen and K. C. Schrøder (eds), *Informal Learning and Digital Media*, Cambridge Scholars, Newcastle, UK, 2008, p. 218.

49   L. Lessig, 'How creativity is being strangled by the law', *TED Talks*, Mar. 2007 (posted Nov. 2007), <www.ted.com/index.php/talks/larry_lessig_says_the_law_is_strangling_creativity.html>.

50   H. Jenkins, 'Photoshop for democracy', *Technology Review*, 4 Jun. 2004, <www.technologyreview.com/biomedicine/13648/>. See also: Jenkins, *Convergence Culture*, pp. 217–50.

51   Lankshear and Knobel, *New Literacies*, pp. 211, 244.

52   H. Rheingold, 'Vision of the future', paper presented to Education.au, 2 Oct. 2007, <www.educationau.edu.au/jahia/Jahia/pid/521>.

53   R. W. Burniske, *Literacy in the Digital Age*, 2nd edn., Corwin, Thousand Oaks, CA, pp. 4, 61–77.

54   T. S. Kazan, 'Braving the body: Embodiment and (cyber-)texts', in J. Lockard and M. Pegrum (eds), *Brave New Classrooms: Democratic Education and the Internet*, Peter Lang, New York, 2007, p. 264.

55   M. Warschauer, *Technology and Social Inclusion: Rethinking the Digital Divide*, MIT Press, Cambridge, MA, 2003, pp. 117–18; M. Warschauer, *Laptops and Literacy: Learning in the Wireless Classroom*, Teachers College Press, New York, 2006, p. 4.

56   'Internet world users by language: Top 10 languages', *Internet World Stats: Usage and Population Statistics*, 31 Mar. 2009, <www.internetworldstats.com/stats7.htm>.

57   G. Dudeney, 'The Luddite codex', *That'SLife*, 26 May 2009, <slife.dudeney.com/?p=238>; G. Dudeney, 'Trainer fail!', *That'SLife*, 27 May 2009, <slife.dudeney.com/?p=240>. These terms come originally from Mike Sansone who, however, uses them in a slightly different sense; see for example, M. Sansone, 'Hey teachers! Your "digital natives" still need you', *ConverStations*, 2 Oct. 2008, <www.converstations.com/2008/10/hey-teachers-yo.html>.

58   M. Prensky, 'Programming is the new literacy', *Edutopia*, Feb. 2008, <www.edutopia.org/programming-the-new-literacy>.

59   Beason, *Eyes Before Ease*, p. 252.

60   J. Sutherland, 'Cn u txt?', *The Guardian*, 11 Nov. 2002, <www.guardian.co.uk/technology/2002/nov/11/mobilephones2>.

61   J. Humphrys, 'I h8 txt msgs: How texting is wrecking our language', *Daily Mail*, 24 Sep. 2007, <www.dailymail.co.uk/news/article-483511/I-h8-txt-msgs-How-texting-wrecking-language.html>.

62   A. Lenhart, S. Arafeh, A. Smith and A. Rankin Macgill, *Writing, Technology and Teens*, Pew Internet & American Life Project, Washington, 24 Apr. 2008, <www.pewinternet.org/Reports/2008/Writing-Technology-and-Teens.aspx>; Crystal, *Txtng*, pp. 152–3.

63   Crystal, *Txtng*, p. 41. See also: C. Snowden, 'Cstng A pwr4l spLL: D evOLshn f SMS', in A. Kavoori and N. Arceneaux (eds), *The Cell Phone Reader: Essays in Social Transformation*, Peter Lang, New York, 2006, esp. pp. 115–18.

64   D. McKnight, *Beyond Right and Left: New Politics and the Culture Wars*, Allen & Unwin, Crows Nest, NSW, 2005, p. 142.

65   U. Clark cited in Snyder, *The Literacy Wars*, p. 183.

66   M. W. Apple, *Education and Power*, 2nd edn., Routledge, New York, 1995; M. W. Apple, *Teachers and Texts: A Political Economy of Class and Gender Relations in Education*, Routledge, New York, 1986.

67   Leadbeater, *We-Think*, p. 147.

68   Johnson, Levine and Smith, *The Horizon Report: 2008 Australia–New Zealand Edition*, p. 3. See also: Strategic ICT Advisory Service, Department of Education, Employment and Workplace Relations [Australia], *Collaboration in Teaching and Learning*, Education.au, Dulwich, SA, 2009, pp. 29–30, <www.educationau.edu.au/jahia/webdav/site/myjahiasite/shared/papers/2009_SICTAS_CTL.pdf>.

69   Snyder, *The Literacy Wars*.

70   See for example, J. Milroy and L. Milroy, *Authority in Language: Investigating Language Prescription and Standardisation*, Routledge, London, 1985; M. Pegrum, 'And on the eighth day: The struggle for linguistic organization', *Bad Subjects*, vol. 65, Jan. 2004, <bad.eserver.org/issues/2004/65/pegrum.html/>; R. Wardhaugh, *Proper English: Myths and Misunderstandings about Language*, Blackwell, Malden, MA, 1999.

71   K. Donnelly, 'English goes back to basics', *The Australian*, 17 Oct. 2008, <www.theaustralian.news.com.au/story/0,25197,24508876-5015664,00.html>.

72   J. Jarvis, *What Would Google Do?*, Collins Business, New York, 2009, p. 214.

73   A. Sfard, 'On two metaphors for learning and the dangers of choosing just one', *Educational Researcher*, vol. 27, no. 2, pp. 4–13.

74   G. Motteram, 'Social computing and teacher education: An agenda for course development', *Innovation in Language Learning and Teaching*, vol. 3, no. 1, pp. 83–97.

75   G. Salmon, *E-tivities: The Key to Active Online Learning*, Kogan Page, London, 2002, p. 90.

76   M. Prensky, *Digital Game-Based Learning*, Paragon House, St. Paul, MN, 2007, p. 17.

77   Kip Leland cited in M. Prensky, '"Engage me or enrage me": What today's learners demand', *EDUCAUSE Review*, vol. 40, no. 5, Sep./Oct. 2005, p. 60, <net.educause.edu/ir/library/pdf/erm0553.pdf>.

78   Naomi Baron cited in S. Carlson, 'The net generation goes to college', *The Chronicle of Higher Education*, 7 Oct. 2005, <chronicle.com/free/v52/i07/07a03401.htm>.

79   See for example, A. Frean, 'White bread for young minds, says University of Brighton professor', *The Times*, 14 Jan. 2008, <technology.timesonline.co.uk/tol/news/tech_and_web/the_web/article3182091.ece>.

80   Brabazon, *Digital Hemlock*, pp. 151–2.

81   T. Brabazon, 'Won't get Googled again: Searching for an education', in Lockard and Pegrum (eds), *Brave New Classrooms*, p. 163.

82   R. G. Ragsdale (with reference to J. R. Eggers and J. F. Wedman), *Permissible Computing in Education: Values, Assumptions, and Needs*, Praeger, New York, 1988, p. 228; Ragsdale (with reference to Bob Davis), *Permissible Computing*, p. 243. See also: A. R. Clayton-Pedersen with N. O'Neill, 'Curricula designed to meet 21st-century expectations', in D. G. Oblinger and J. L. Oblinger (eds), *Educating the Net Generation*, EDUCAUSE, pp. 9.1–9.16, <net.educause.edu/ir/library/pdf/pub7101i.pdf>.

83   D. Gibbs and K.-L. Krause, 'Metaphor and meaning: Values in a virtual world', in D. Gibbs and K.-L. Krause (eds), *Cyberlines: Languages and Cultures of the Internet*, James Nicholas, Albert Park, Vic, 2000, p. 38.

84   J. Pegg, C. Reading and M. Williams, *Partnerships in ICT Learning Study: Full Report*, Department of Education, Science and Training [Australia], Canberra, 2007, p. 10, <www.deewr.gov.au/Schooling/DigitalEducationRevolution/Documents/pictl_full_report1.pdf>.

85   V. Stevens (with reference to Women of Web 2.0), 'Jobs that haven't been invented yet', *Webhead Link*, 8 Jan. 2007, <webheadlink.wordpress.com/2007/01/08/jobs-that-havent-been-invented-yet/>. In a slightly different formulation, Karl Fisch states that: 'We are currently preparing students for jobs that don't yet exist…Using technologies that haven't been

invented...In order to solve problems we don't even know are problems yet'; see K. Fisch, 'Did you know?', PowerPoint presentation at Arapahoe High School Faculty Meeting, 2006, <thefischbowl.blogspot.com/2006/08/did-you-know.html>.

86 Warschauer, *Technology and Social Inclusion;* C. Haythornthwaite, 'Digital divide and e-learning', in R. Andrews and C. Haythornthwaite (eds), *The Sage Handbook of E-learning Research*, Sage, London, 2007, pp. 97–118.

4 – Many selves: A social lens

1 Tapscott, *Growing Up Digital;* Tapscott, *Grown Up Digital.* Other authors use slightly different terms and slightly different birth years.

2 C. Aldrich, *Learning by Doing: A Comprehensive Guide to Simulations, Computer Games, and Pedagogy in E-learning and Other Educational Experiences*, Pfeiffer, San Francisco, 2005, p. xxix.

3 D. Tapscott and A. D. Williams, *Wikinomics: How Mass Collaboration Changes Everything*, Portfolio, New York, p. 47. See also: Tapscott, *Growing Up Digital*, pp. 1–2; Tapscott, *Grown Up Digital*, pp. 2, 28.

4 Australian Communications and Media Authority, *Telecommunications Today. Report 6: Internet Activity and Content*, Canberra, 2008, pp. 7, 17–19, <www.acma.gov.au/webwr/_assets/main/lib310210/report_6_telecommunications_today.pdf>; E. J. Hesper, *Digital Inclusion: An Analysis of Social Disadvantage and the Information Society*, Department for Communities and Local Government [UK], London, 2008, <www.communities.gov.uk/documents/communities/pdf/digitalinclusionanalysis>; N. Selwyn and K. Facer, *Beyond the Digital Divide: Rethinking Digital Inclusion for the 21st Century*, Futurelab, Bristol, 2007, pp. 18–19, <www.futurelab.org.uk/resources/documents/opening_education/Digital_Divide.pdf>.

5 S. Bennett, K. Maton and L. Kervin, 'The "digital natives" debate: A critical review of the evidence', *British Journal of Educational Technology*, vol. 39, no. 5, 2008, pp. 775–86; CIBER, *Information Behaviour of the Researcher of the Future*, 11 Jan. 2008, <www.jisc.ac.uk/media/documents/programmes/reppres/gg_final_keynote_11012008.pdf>; S. C. Herring, 'Questioning the generational divide: Technological exoticism and adult constructions of online youth identity', in Buckingham (ed.), *Youth, Identity, and Digital Media*, pp. 71–92, <www.mitpressjournals.org/doi/pdf/10.1162/dmal.9780262524834.071>; G. Kennedy, B. Dalgarno, S. Bennett, T. Judd, K. Gray and R. Chang, 'Immigrants and natives: Investigating differences between staff and students' use of technology', paper presented at ASCILITE 2008, Melbourne, <www.ascilite.org.au/conferences/melbourne08/procs/kennedy.pdf>; K.-L. Krause, 'Who is the e-generation and how are they faring in higher education?', in Lockard and Pegrum (eds), *Brave New Classrooms*, pp. 125–39; Strategic ICT Advisory Service, *Collaboration in Teaching and Learning*, pp. 5, 26–8.

6 See the results of the 2004 and 2006 EDUCAUSE Center for Applied Research (ECAR) Studies, as reported in: R. B. Kravik, 'Convenience, communications, and control: How students use technology', in Oblinger and Oblinger (eds), *Educating the Net Generation*, pp. 7.8–7.9, 7.17, <net.educause.edu/ir/library/pdf/pub7101g.pdf>; R. N. Katz, *Key Findings: The ECAR Study of Undergraduate Students and Information Technology, 2006*, EDUCAUSE, Dec. 2006, p. 4, <net.educause.edu/ir/library/pdf/EKF/EKF0607.pdf>.

7 R. Boyes, 'And this is me on Facebook...helping with brain surgery', *The Times*, 18 Aug. 2008, <www.timesonline.co.uk/tol/news/world/europe/article4560908.ece>.

8 Press Association, 'Juror shares trial details on Facebook', *The Guardian*, 24 Nov. 2008, <www.guardian.co.uk/uk/2008/nov/24/ukcrime1>.

9 Jenny Sundén cited in d. boyd, 'Why youth ♥ social network sites: The role of networked publics in teenage social life', in Buckingham (ed.), *Youth, Identity, and Digital Media*, p. 129, <www.mitpressjournals.org/doi/pdf/10.1162/dmal.9780262524834.119>.

10 F. Stalder, 'Bourgeois anarchism and authoritarian democracies', *First Monday*, vol. 13, no. 7, 7 Jul. 2008, <firstmonday.org/htbin/cgiwrap/bin/ojs/index.php/fm/article/view/2077/1989>.

11   Cf. Kress, 'Visual and verbal modes of representation', p. 72.

12   S. Boxer, 'Introduction', in S. Boxer (ed.), *Ultimate Blogs: Masterworks from the Wild Web*, Vintage, New York, 2008, p. xv.

13   S. Stern, 'Producing sites, exploring identities: Youth online authorship', in Buckingham (ed.), *Youth, Identity, and Digital Media*, esp. pp. 103–4, <www.mitpressjournals.org/doi/ pdf/10.1162/dmal.9780262524834.095>.

14   L. Lessig, *Code Version 2.0*, Basic Books, New York, 2006, p. 20, <codev2.cc/ download+remix/>.

15   M. C. Larsen, 'Understanding social networking: On young people's construction and co-construction of identity online', paper presented at Internet Research 8.0: Let's Play, Vancouver, 17–20 Oct. 2007, <www.ell.aau.dk/fileadmin/user_upload/documents/staff/ Malene_Larsen_-_Documents/Paper_Malene_Charlotte_Larsen_REVISED_version_ Sep07.pdf>; Stern, 'Producing sites, exploring identities', esp. pp. 106–8.

16   Stern, 'Producing sites, exploring identities', pp. 108, 110–11. See also: J. Cabiria, 'Virtual world and real world permeability: Transference of positive benefits for marginalized gay and lesbian populations', *Journal of Virtual Worlds Research*, vol. 1, no. 1, <journals.tdl.org/ jvwr/article/view/284/215>; A. Thomas, *Youth Online: Identity and Literacy in the Digital Age*, Peter Lang, New York, 2007, p. 189.

17   A. Chester and D. Bretherton, 'Impression management and identity online', in A. N. Joinson, K. Y. A. McKenna, T. Postmes and U. D. Reips (eds), *The Oxford Handbook of Internet Psychology*, Oxford University Press, Oxford, 2007, esp. pp. 233–5; J. P. Marshall, 'Gender in online communication', in J. Coiro, M. Knobel, C. Lankshear and D. J. Leu (eds), *Handbook of Research on New Literacies*, Lawrence Erlbaum, New York, 2008, p. 502.

18   See for example, Au, *The Making of Second Life*, pp. 201–7; M. Kizelshteyn, 'Therapy and the metaverse: Second Life and the changing conditions of therapy for convalescent and chronically ill users', *Washington University Undergraduate Research Digest*, vol. 4, no. 1, Fall 2008, pp. 17–26, <www.turtlethink.com/WUURD%202008_Kizelshteyn.pdf>.

19   On 'egocentric networks', see: boyd, 'Friends, Friendsters, and Top 8'.

20   Lenhart et al., *Teens and Social Media*. On blogging, see also: C. Ryan, 'Blogging boosts your social life: Research', *ABC News* [Aus.], 3 Mar. 2008, <www.abc.net.au/news/ stories/2008/03/03/2178512.htm>. On gaming, see also: F. Caron, 'Study squashes myth of gamer as antisocial Comic Book Guy', *Ars Technica*, 22 Oct. 2008, <arstechnica. com/news.ars/post/20081022-study-squashes-myth-of-gamer-as-antisocial-comic-book-guy.html>; A. McFarlane, 'Learning and lessons from the world of games and play', in Andrews and Haythornthwaite (eds), *The Sage Handbook of E-learning Research*, p. 120.

21   A. Madrigal, 'Mourning the internet famous: Randy Pausch's distributed funeral', *Wired*, 29 Jul. 2008, <www.wired.com/culture/lifestyle/news/2008/07/distributed_funeral>.

22   M. Castells, M. Fernández-Ardèvol, J. Linchuan Qiu and A. Sey, *Mobile Communication and Society: A Global Perspective*, MIT Press, Cambridge, MA, 2007, p. 144. On networked individualism, see for example, B. Wellman, A. Quan-Haase, J. Boase, W. Chen, K. Hampton, I. Isla de Diaz and K. Miyata, 'The social affordances of the internet for networked individualism', *Journal of Computer-Mediated Communication*, vol. 8, no. 3, 2003, <jcmc.indiana.edu/vol8/issue3/wellman.html>.

23   M. Ito, H. Horst, M. Bittanti, d. boyd, B. Herr-Stephenson, P. G. Lange, C. J. Pascoe, L. Robinson et al., *Living and Learning with New Media: Summary of Findings from the Digital Youth Project*, The MacArthur Foundation, Chicago, Nov. 2008, p. 1, <www.macfound.org/atf/cf/%7BB0386CE3-8B29-4162-8098-E466FB856794%7D/ DML_ETHNOG_ WHITEPAPER.PDF>; C. Lampe, N. Ellison and C. Steinfield, 'A Face(book) in the crowd: Social searching vs. social browsing', paper presented at CSCW'06, Banff, Canada, 4–8 Nov. 2006, <https://www.msu.edu/~steinfie/ CSCW_Facebook.pdf>; Northwestern University, 'Tracking the digital traces of social networks', *e! Science News*, 14 Feb. 2009, <esciencenews.com/articles/2009/02/14/ tracking.digital.traces.social.networks>.

24 See for example, R. Scruton, 'Can virtual life take over from real life?', *The Times*, 16 Nov. 2008, <technology.timesonline.co.uk/tol/news/tech_and_web/the_web/article5139532.ece>.

25 H. Mackay, *Advance Australia…Where?*, Hachette, Sydney, 2008, p. 100.

26 d. boyd, 'Teen socialization practices in networked publics', paper presented at the MacArthur Forum, Palo Alto, CA, 23 Apr. 2008, <www.danah.org/papers/talks/MacArthur2008.html>. See also the discussion of phatic communication in G. Stald, 'Mobile identity: Youth, identity, and mobile communication media', in Buckingham (ed.), *Youth, Identity, and Digital Media*, esp. pp. 151–2, 155, <www.mitpressjournals.org/doi/pdf/10.1162/dmal.9780262524834.143>; R. Ling, *New Tech, New Ties: How Mobile Communication is Reshaping Social Cohesion*, MIT Press, Cambridge, MA, 2008, pp. 168–9.

27 The term 'ambient intimacy' was coined by blogger Leisa Reichelt, as cited in J. Jarvis, 'Why Twitter is the canary in the news coalmine', *The Guardian*, 19 May 2008, <www.guardian.co.uk/media/2008/may/19/digitalmedia.socialnetworking>. See also: T. O'Reilly and S. Milstein, *The Twitter Book*, O'Reilly, Sebastopol, CA, 2009, pp. 9, 167. The term 'social peripheral vision' was coined by Jyri Engeström, co-founder of Jaiku. See for example, J. Engeström, 'Nodal points', paper presented at The Web and Beyond, 2008, <www.youtube.com/watch?v=SiWjAVcWK4g>.

28 See for example, S. Ewing, J. Thomas and J. Schiessl, *CCi Digital Futures Report: The Internet in Australia*, ARC Centre of Excellence for Creative Industries and Innovation, Swinburne University of Technology, Melbourne, Jul. 2008, esp. pp. 12–14, <researchbank.swinburne.edu.au/vital/access/manager/Repository/swin:8506>; T. L. M. Kennedy, A. Smith, A. T. Wells and B. Wellman, *Networked Families*, Pew Internet & American Life Project, Washington, 19 Oct. 2008, esp. pp. iii–iv, 25–8, <www.pewinternet.org/Reports/2008/Networked-Families.aspx>; Ling, *New Tech, New Ties*.

29 T. Byron, *Safer Children in a Digital World: The Report of the Byron Review*, DCSF Publications, Nottingham, 2008, p. 2. See also: boyd, 'Why youth ♥ social network sites', pp. 134–7.

30 Here, online social networks diverge from mobile phone contacts. While both help to reinforce close ties, mobile phones are not used in the same way to maintain or reinforce weak ties. See: Ling, *New Tech, New Ties*, pp. 175–87.

31 Benkler (with reference to Manuel Castells and Barry Wellman), *The Wealth of Networks*, pp. 15–16; see also pp. 363–9.

32 N. B. Ellison, C. Steinfield and C. Lampe, 'The benefits of Facebook "friends:" Social capital and college students' use of online social network sites', *Journal of Computer-Mediated Communication*, vol. 12, no. 4, 2007, <jcmc.indiana.edu/vol12/issue4/ellison.html>.

33 P. Rutledge, 'Why LinkedIn works: The strength of weak ties', *Psychology Today Blogs*, 15 Mar. 2009, <blogs.psychologytoday.com/blog/positively-media/200903/why-linkedin-works-the-strength-weak-ties>.

34 C. Rosen, 'Virtual friendship and the new narcissism', *The New Atlantis*, vol. 17, Summer 2007, p. 27, <www.thenewatlantis.com/docLib/TNA17-Rosen.pdf>.

35 M. T. Whitty, 'Liberating or debilitating? An examination of romantic relationships, sexual relationships and friendships on the net', *Computers in Human Behaviour*, vol. 24, 2008, p. 1837.

36 *Sex and Tech: Results from a Survey of Teens and Young Adults*, The National Campaign to Prevent Teen and Unplanned Pregnancy, Washington, 2008, <www.thenationalcampaign.org/sextech/PDF/SexTech_Summary.pdf>.

37 M. Kanuga and W. D. Rosenfeld, 'Adolescent sexuality and the internet: The good, the bad, and the URL', *Journal of Pediatric and Adolescent Gynecology*, vol. 17, no. 2, 2004, pp. 117–24.

38 Kanuga and Rosenfeld (with reference to D. Zillmann), 'Adolescent sexuality and the internet', p. 120.

39 See for example, M. Ahmed, 'Teen "sexting" craze leading to child porn arrests in US', *The Times*, 14 Jan. 2009, <technology.timesonline.co.uk/tol/news/tech_and_web/article5516511.ece>.

40 L. A. Adamic and N. Glance, 'The political blogosphere and the 2004 U.S. election:

Divided they blog', paper presented at the International Conference on Knowledge Discovery and Data Mining, Chicago, 21–25 Aug. 2005, <portal.acm.org/citation.cfm?id= 1134271.1134277>; M. Thelwall, 'Homophily in MySpace', *Journal of the American Society for Information Science and Technology*, vol. 60, no. 2, 2009, pp. 219–31. Interestingly, though, gender homophily was not found in Thelwall's study.

41 Carr, *The Big Switch*, p. 160.

42 D. Weinberger, 'Echo chambers = democracy', in A. Fine, M. L. Sifry, A. Rasiej and J. Levy (eds), *Rebooting America: Ideas for Redesigning American Democracy for the Internet Age*, Personal Democracy Press, 2008, pp. 33–4, <rebooting.personaldemocracy.com/files/ DavidWeinberger.pdf>.

43 boyd, 'Friends, Friendsters, and Top 8'; d. boyd, 'Social media is here to stay...Now what?', paper presented at the Microsoft Research Tech Fest, Redmond, WA, 26 Feb. 2009, <www.danah.org/papers/talks/MSRTechFest2009.html>.

44 A YouTube search for the term 'Bus Uncle' will turn up many relevant results, which are too numerous to list here. For another account of this story, see: Zittrain, *The Future of the Internet*, p. 211.

45 Palfrey and Gasser, *Born Digital*, pp. 19–20.

46 On privacy and surveillance, see: Abelson, Ledeen and Lewis, *Blown to Bits;* E. Dyson, 'How loss of privacy may mean loss of security', *Scientific American*, vol. 299, no. 3, Sep. 2008, <www.sciam.com/article.cfm?id=how-loss-of-privacy-may-mean-loss-of-security>; D. J. Solove, *The Future of Reputation: Gossip, Rumor, and Privacy on the Internet*, Yale University Press, New Haven, CT, 2007.

47 Boyes, 'And this is me on Facebook...'; A. Moses, 'Your Facebook secrets: Jobs under threat', *The Sydney Morning Herald*, 2 Apr. 2009, <www.smh.com.au/news/technology/ your-facebook-secrets-jobs-under-threat/2009/04/02/1238261699036.html>; A. Moses, 'Facebook discipline may be illegal: Expert', *The Sydney Morning Herald*, 3 Apr. 2009, <www.smh.com.au/news/technology/facebook-discipline-may-be-illegal-expert/2009/04/03/1238261779328.html>.

48 On vengeance blogs, see: D. Smith, 'Revenge is a dish best served...online', *The Observer*, 27 Apr. 2008, <www.guardian.co.uk/technology/2008/apr/27/internet.blogging>. On Chinese human flesh search engines, see: Bai Xu and Ji Shaoting, '"Human flesh search engine": An internet lynching?', *Xinhua/China View*, 4 Jul. 2008, <news.xinhuanet.com/english/2008-07/04/content_8491087.htm>; H. Fletcher, 'Human flesh search engines: Chinese vigilantes that hunt victims on the web', *The Times*, 25 Jun. 2008, <technology.timesonline.co.uk/tol/ news/tech_and_web/article4213681.ece>; 'Virtual carnivores', *The Economist*, 2 Oct. 2008, <www.economist.com/world/asia/displaystory.cfm?story_id=12342705&fsrc>.

49 Scott McNealy cited in P. Sprenger, 'Sun on privacy: "Get over it"', *Wired*, 26 Jan. 1999, <www.wired.com/politics/law/news/1999/01/17538>.

50 'Everybody does it', *The Economist*, 2 Jan. 2009, <www.economist.com/science/ displaystory.cfm?story_id=12842387&fsrc>.

51 Jeff Jarvis cited in D. Smith, 'What happens when bloggers bare all then get caught in the brutal blowback', *The Observer*, 25 May 2008, <www.guardian.co.uk/ media/2008/may/25/digitalmedia.blogging>; a similar idea is expressed in 'Everybody does it'. See also: J. Jarvis, 'Openness and the internet', *Business Week*, 8 May 2009, <www.businessweek.com/managing/content/may2009/ca2009058_754247. htm?chan=careers_managing+index+page_top+stories>.

52 M. Simun, 'Going loca: Privacy in a digital world', *Digital Natives*, 15 Jul. 2008, <blogs.law.harvard.edu/digitalnatives/2008/07/15/going-loca-privacy-in-a-digital-world/>.

53 J. Cassell and M. Cramer, 'High tech or high risk: Moral panics about girls online', in T. McPherson, *Digital Youth, Innovation, and the Unexpected*, MIT Press, Cambridge, MA, 2008, pp. 61, 64, <www.mitpressjournals.org/doi/pdf/10.1162/ dmal.9780262633598.053>.

54 Charles Acland cited in K. Crawford and G. Goggin, 'Handsome devils: Mobile

imaginings of youth culture', *Global Media Journal* (Australian edn.), vol. 1, no. 1, 2008, p. 6, <stc.uws.edu.au/gmjau/iss1_2008/pdf/crawford_goggin_GMJAU_2008.pdf>.

55   Crawford and Goggin, 'Handsome devils', pp. 4–5.

56   Internet Safety Technical Task Force, *Enhancing Child Safety and Online Technologies: Final Report of the Internet Safety Technical Task Force to the Multi-State Working Group on Social Networking of State Attorneys General of the United States*, Berkman Center for Internet and Society at Harvard University, 31 Dec. 2008, pp. 5, 18–19 & Appendix C, pp. 29–31, <cyber.law.harvard.edu/pubrelease/isttf/>. Note that most data and statistics quoted in this section come from US research.

57   ibid., Appendix C, p. 10; H. Lewis, 'The dangers of internet censorship', *The Boston Globe*, 5 Nov. 2008, <www.boston.com/bostonglobe/editorial_opinion/oped/articles/2008/11/05/the_dangers_of_internet_censorship/>.

58   Cassell and Cramer, 'High tech or high risk', pp. 54, 56–7.

59   danah boyd (with reference to Barry Glassner), in d. boyd and H. Jenkins, 'Discussion: MySpace and Deleting Online Predators Act (DOPA)' [interview by S. Wright], *MIT Tech Talk*, 26 May 2006, <www.danah.org/papers/MySpaceDOPA.html> (full version).

60   Internet Safety Technical Task Force, *Enhancing Child Safety*, Appendix C, p. 15. See also: Cassell and Cramer, 'High tech or high risk', pp. 55, 58; Tapscott, *Grown Up Digital*, p. 222.

61   Internet Safety Technical Task Force, *Enhancing Child Safety*, pp. 13–16.

62   ibid., p. 17. A recent European survey conducted for Microsoft puts the figure at 29 per cent, though there are considerable differences between countries; see: Microsoft, '29% of European teenagers are victims of online bullying', *Microsoft EMEA Press Centre*, 10 Feb. 2009, <www.microsoft.com/emea/presscentre/pressreleases/OnlinebullyingPR_100209.mspx>.

63   J. Juvonen and E. F. Gross, 'Extending the school grounds?—Bullying experiences in cyberspace', *The Journal of School Health*, vol. 78, no. 9, Sep. 2008, pp. 496–505.

64   Internet Safety Technical Task Force, *Enhancing Child Safety*, Appendix C, p. 12.

65   Juvonen and Gross, 'Extending the school grounds?', p. 500; A. Lenhart, *Cyberbullying and Online Teens*, Data Memo, Pew Internet & American Life Project, Washington, 27 Jun. 2007, <www.pewinternet.org/Reports/2007/Cyberbullying.aspx>.

66   Juvonen and Gross, 'Extending the school grounds?', p. 503.

67   Australian Communications and Media Authority, *Telecommunications Today: Report 6*, p. 28.

68   N. Higginbottom and B. Packham, 'Student cracks government's $84m porn filter', *News.com.au*, 26 Aug. 2007, <www.news.com.au/story/0,23599,22304224-2,00.html>.

69   The tendency for filtering software to mistake gay and lesbian sites for pornography is noted in J. Zittrain and J. Palfrey, 'Internet filtering: The politics and mechanisms of control', in R. Deibert, J. Palfrey, R. Rohozinski and J. Zittrain (eds), *Access Denied: The Practice and Policy of Global Internet Filtering*, MIT Press, Cambridge, MA, 2008, p. 47, <opennet.net/accessdenied>.

70   Judge Lowell A. Reed, Jr, of the US District Court for the Eastern District of Pennsylvania, cited in Abelson, Ledeen and Lewis, *Blown to Bits*, p. 249.

71   H. Gilmore, 'Web porn software filter takes biggest hit', *The Sydney Morning Herald*, 17 Feb. 2008, <www.smh.com.au/news/technology/web-porn-filter-takes-biggest-hit/2008/02/16/1202760663247.html>.

72   Internet Safety Technical Task Force, *Enhancing Child Safety*, pp. 7, 16, 20 & Appendix C, pp. 39, 43–4.

73   ibid., p. 7.

74   Holly Doel-Mackaway cited in C. Jacobs, 'Cyber-libertarians love their children too', *Electronic Frontiers Australia*, 20 Feb. 2009, <www.efa.org.au/2009/02/20/cyber-libertarians-love-their-children-too/>.

75   Tom Wood cited in Higginbottom and Packham, 'Student cracks government's $84m porn filter'.

76   For examples of promising educational initiatives, see the Australian Communications and
      Media Authority's *Cybersmart* initiative, <www.cybersmart.gov.au>; in the EU, Insafe's
      annual *Safer Internet Day*, <www.saferinternet.org/ww/en/pub/insafe/sid.htm>; and in
      the UK, the Child Exploitation and Online Protection Centre's *Thinkuknow* initiative,
      <www.thinkuknow.co.uk>. In May 2009, the Australian Government announced that a
      Youth Advisory Group consisting of 305 11 to 17-year-olds had been formed to provide
      advice on its online safety plans; see: 'Youth to advise government on cyber-bullying and
      cyber-threats', *Senator the Hon Stephen Conroy*, 4 May 2009, <www.minister.dbcde.gov.au/
      media/media_releases/2009/031>. Such an initiative is certainly to be welcomed but its
      value will be limited if in fact the government has already decided on filtering as its key
      safety strategy; see Chapter 5 for further discussion.

77   P. E. Agre, 'Welcome to the always-on world', *IEEE Spectrum*, vol. 38, no. 1, Jan. 2001,
      pp. 10–13.

78   Patricia Cranton cited in G. I. Maeroff, *A Classroom of One: How Online Learning is
      Changing Our Schools and Colleges*, Palgrave Macmillan, New York, 2003, p. 68.

79   L. Low, '10 reasons handheld learning rocks', *Mobile Learning*, 8 Mar. 2007,
      <mlearning.wordpress.com/2007/03/08/10-reasons-handheld-learning-rocks/>.

80   *Information overload:* for example, J. Richards, 'Tech firms act to counter "information
      overload"', *The Times*, 16 Jun. 2008, <technology.timesonline.co.uk/tol/news/
      tech_and_web/article4148242.ece>; *information fatigue syndrome:* David Lewis cited in
      J. Naish, *Enough: Breaking Free from the World of More*, Hodder & Stoughton, London,
      2008, p. 17; *news fatigue:* The Associated Press and the Context-Based Research Group,
      A New Model for News: Studying the Deep Structure of Young-Adult News Consumption,
      Associated Press, Jun. 2008, <www.ap.org/newmodel.pdf>; *infomania:* Glenn Wilson's
      study for Hewlett-Packard, cited in '"Infomania" worse than marijuana', *BBC News*,
      22 Apr. 2005, <news.bbc.co.uk/2/hi/uk_news/4471607.stm> and in Naish, *Enough*,
      p. 18; *information obesity:* A. Whitworth, *Information Obesity*, Chandos, Oxford, 2009;
      infobesity: John Naish's own term in Naish, *Enough*, p. 25.

81   N. Zeldes, D. Sward and S. Louchheim (with reference to V. Gonzalez and G. Mark
      for the figure of 3 minutes' uninterrupted work), 'Infomania: Why we can't afford
      to ignore it any longer', *First Monday*, vol. 12, no. 8, 6 Aug. 2007, <firstmonday.org/
      htbin/cgiwrap/bin/ojs/index.php/fm/article/view/1973/1848>.

82   M. Madden and S. Jones, *Networked Workers*, Pew Internet & American Life Project,
      Washington, 24 Sep. 2008, <www.pewinternet.org/Reports/2008/Networked-
      Workers.aspx>.

83   Naomi Baron refers to this as 'volume control' in N. S. Baron, *Always On: Language in
      an Online and Mobile World*, Oxford University Press, New York, 2008, pp. 5–6, 31–44.

84   Australian Communications and Media Authority, *Telecommunications Today: Report 6*,
      pp. 26–7; Ewing, Thomas and Schiessl, *CCi Digital Futures Report*, p. 21.

85   Nielsen Online, *Aussies Ditch the Desktop in Favour of Wireless Technology*, News Release,
      2 Mar. 2009, <blog.nielsen.com/nielsenwire/wp-content/uploads/2009/03/itrpt-mr-
      mar092.pdf>.

86   On the UK, see: L. Peel, 'Hello? I'm on the internet – and watching the television', *The
      Times*, 14 Aug. 2008, <business.timesonline.co.uk/tol/business/industry_sectors/media/
      article4526635.ece>; on the US, see: V. Rideout, D. F. Roberts and U. G. Foehr,
      Generation M: Media in the Lives of 8–18 Year-Olds: Executive Summary, The Kaiser Family
      Foundation, Menlo Park, CA, Mar. 2005, pp. 6, 23, <www.kff.org/entmedia/upload/
      Executive-Summary-Generation-M-Media-in-the-Lives-of-8-18-Year-olds.pdf>.

87   Jenkins et al., *Confronting the Challenges of Participatory Culture*, p. 35.

88   Baron, *Always On*, pp. 36–9, 217–18; W. Kirn, 'The autumn of the multitaskers', *The
      Atlantic*, Nov. 2007, <www.theatlantic.com/doc/200711/multitasking>; Palfrey and
      Gasser, *Born Digital*, p. 191; G. Small and G. Vorgan, *iBrain: Surviving the Technological
      Alteration of the Modern Mind*, Collins, New York, 2008, pp. 32–4, 67–9, 137; Tapscott,

Grown Up Digital, pp. 106–9; C. Wallis, 'The multitasking generation', *Time*, 19 Mar. 2006, <www.time.com/time/magazine/article/0,9171,1174696,00.html>.

89 Bruce Friedman cited in N. Carr, 'Is Google making us stupid?', *The Atlantic*, Jul./Aug. 2008, <www.theatlantic.com/doc/200807/google>. See also: N. Carr, *The Shallows: Mind, Memory and Media in an Age of Instant Information*, W. W. Norton (forthcoming).

90 Naish, *Enough*, pp. 244–5.

91 Stone, 'Fine dining with mobile devices'. See also: L. Stone, *Linda Stone's Thoughts on Attention and Specifically, Continuous Partial Attention*, 2007, <www.lindastone.net>.

92 K. Kelly, 'What technologies do you reject?', *KK: Help Wanted*, 2 Mar. 2004, <www.kk.org/helpwanted/archives/000324.php>.

93 L. Lessig, 'Lessig blog: Closed until June', *Lessig 2.0*, 2 May 2008, <www.lessig.org/blog/2008/05/lessig_blog_closed_until_june.html>.

94 d. boyd, 'Email sabbatical has begun', *Apophenia*, 11 Dec. 2008, <www.zephoria.org/thoughts/archives/2008/12/11/email_sabbatica.html>.

95 Stone, 'Fine dining with mobile devices'.

5 – Many stories: A sociopolitical lens

1 Rheingold, *Smart Mobs*, pp. xi–xvii.

2 'Outcry in SA over "racist" video', *BBC News*, 27 Feb. 2008, <news.bbc.co.uk/2/hi/africa/7267027.stm>; 'South Africa dorm closed over urine stew video', *CNN.com*, 27 May 2008, <edition.cnn.com/2008/WORLD/africa/05/27/safrica.dorm/index.html>; M. Karim, 'South Africa: The Free State racist video saga', *Global Voices*, 9 Mar. 2008, <globalvoicesonline.org/2008/03/09/the-free-state-racist-video-saga/>. With its complex recent history, South Africa is not necessarily regarded as a Western country, but the incident described here is typical of the kinds of racism found in Western contexts.

3 'Policeman's video of intoxicated Aboriginal man put on YouTube', *ABC News* [Aus.], 27 Jan. 2009, <www.abc.net.au/news/stories/2009/01/27/2475226.htm>; 'Police in damage control over "sickening" YouTube video', *ABC News* [Aus.], 27/28 Jan. 2009, <www.abc.net.au/news/stories/2009/01/27/2475729.htm>.

4 Haythornthwaite, 'Digital divide and e-learning', p. 110.

5 See for example, d. boyd, 'Viewing American class divisions through Facebook and MySpace', *Apophenia*, 24 Jun. 2007, <www.zephoria.org/thoughts/archives/2007/06/24/viewing_america.html>; d. boyd, 'Living and learning with social media', paper presented at the Penn State Symposium for Teaching and Learning with Technology, State College, PA, 18 Apr. 2009, <www.danah.org/papers/talks/PennState2009.html>. See also: E. Hargittai, 'Whose space? Differences among users and non-users of social network sites', *Journal of Computer-Mediated Communication*, vol. 13, no. 1, 2007, <jcmc.indiana.edu/vol13/issue1/hargittai.html>; E. Seiter, 'Practicing at home: Computers, pianos, and cultural capital', in McPherson (ed.), *Digital Youth, Innovation, and the Unexpected*, esp. pp. 38–9, <www.mitpressjournals.org/doi/pdf/10.1162/dmal.9780262633598.027>.

6 *Lords of the Blog*, <lordsoftheblog.wordpress.com>.

7 Tim Berners-Lee cited in P. Ghosh, 'Warning sounded on web's future', *BBC News*, 15 Sep. 2008, <news.bbc.co.uk/2/hi/technology/7613201.stm>.

8 T. Brabazon, *The University of Google: Education in the (Post) Information Age*, Ashgate, Aldershot, 2007, pp. 56–7. Brabazon is in fact referring to poverty within the West as much as beyond it, but there is no doubt that the proportion of those who enjoy 'digi-leisure' is far lower in the developing world.

9 D. Sasaki, 'Rising voices: Helping the global population join the global conversation', Announcement for Berkman Luncheon Series, Harvard University, 28 Oct. 2008, <cyber.law.harvard.edu/events/luncheon/2008/10/sasaki>.

10 Bruns, *Blogs, Wikipedia, Second Life, and Beyond*, p. 403; Goldsmith and Wu, *Who Controls the Internet?*, p. 89.

11   Diana Kleiner cited in A. Balakrishnan, 'Reading poetry at Yale...in my sitting room', *The Guardian*, 29 Apr. 2008, <education.guardian.co.uk/egweekly/story/ 0,,2276644,00.html>.

12   J. Wales, 'The wisdom of crowds', *The Guardian*, 22 Jun. 2008, <www.guardian.co.uk/ commentisfree/2008/jun/22/wikipedia.internet>.

13   M. H. McCormick, 'Webmastered: Postcolonialism and the internet', in Lockard and Pegrum (eds), *Brave New Classrooms*, pp. 82–3.

14   The second quote is taken from a set of forums co-organised with Stephen Bax in 2007; see: S. Bax and M. Pegrum, 'Lurking in multicultural online educational forums: "I wasn't invited to the party"', in A. Ragusa (ed.), *Interaction in Communication Technologies and Virtual Learning Environments: Human Factors*, IGI Global, Hershey, PA, 2009.

15   C. Ess, 'Liberal arts and distance education: Can Socratic virtue (ἀρετή) and Confucius' exemplary person (*junzi*) be taught online?', in Lockard and Pegrum (eds), *Brave New Classrooms*, p. 195.

16   In collaborative work with Stephen Bax, I have referred to such mediated intercultural spaces as 'educational third spaces'. For a fuller account of these spaces, please see the wiki page for our ongoing *Third Space in Online Discussion* project at: <e-language.wikispaces.com/mr1>.

17   A. Madrigal, 'Olympic-Torch security troops block Everest bloggers' climb', *Wired*, 30 Apr. 2008, <www.wired.com/culture/lifestyle/news/2008/04/everest_bloggers>.

18   Y. Sánchez, *Generación Y*, <www.desdecuba.com/generaciony/>.

19   A. Loewenstein, *The Blogging Revolution*, Melbourne University Press, Melbourne, 2008, pp. 121, 130.

20   Mark Karstad interviewed in A. Fox, *Absolutely Intercultural 62* [podcast], 25 Jul. 2008, <www.absolutely-intercultural.com/?p=99>.

21   Mi-Jin Kang (Kangdidas) cited in R. Cooper, *Alter Ego: Avatars and their Creators*, Chris Boot, London, 2007, unpag.

22   M. Weaver, 'Social networking sites: Do not pry, says online community', *The Guardian*, 25 Mar. 2009, <www.guardian.co.uk/uk/blog/2009/mar/25/myspace- twitter-facebook-monitoring>.

23   Loewenstein, *The Blogging Revolution*, p. 5.

24   Sam Gregory (with reference to Peter Gabriel), cited in H. Jenkins, 'From Rodney King to Burma: An interview with Witness's Sam Gregory (Part One)', *Confessions of an Aca-Fan*, 31 Mar. 2008, <www.henryjenkins.org/2008/03/from_rodney_king_to_ burma_an_ i.html>.

25   R. Beschizza, 'Why you should give your kids cellphones: Baltimore cop filmed attacking teenager', *Wired*, 13 Feb. 2008, <blog.wired.com/gadgets/2008/02/why-you- should.html>; P. Waldo, 'Must see video', *The Huffington Post*, 15 Feb. 2008, <www.huffingtonpost.com/2008/02/15/must-see-video-huckabee-_n_86739.html>.

26   S. Israel, 'James Karl Buck Twitters his way out of Egypt jailhouse', *Global Neighbourhoods*, 17 Apr. 2008, <redcouch.typepad.com/weblog/2008/04/james-karl-buck.html>; M. Simon, 'Student "Twitters" his way out of Egyptian jail', *CNN.com*, 25 Apr. 2008, <www.cnn.com/2008/TECH/04/25/twitter.buck/index.html>. The student, James Karl Buck, was able to keep his phone and posted later status updates from jail, but it seems the first tweet set in motion the events leading to his release.

27   Rheingold, *Smart Mobs;* Shirky, *Here Comes Everybody*, pp. 164–71.

28   On the Philippines, see: Castells et al., *Mobile Communication and Society*, pp. 186–93; Rheingold, *Smart Mobs*, pp. 157–60. On South Korea, see: Castells et al., *Mobile Communication and Society*, pp. 193–8; H. Rheingold, 'Mobile media and political collective action', in J. E. Katz (ed.), *Handbook of Mobile Communication Studies*, MIT Press, Cambridge, MA, 2008, p. 228. On Spain, see: Castells et al., *Mobile Communication and Society*, pp. 198–202; Rheingold, 'Mobile media and political collective action', pp. 228–9.

29   For a reflective account of the Iranian situation, see: C. Delany, 'Iran, Independence

Day and the limits of online politics', *techPresident*, 5 Jul. 2009, <techpresident.com/blog-entry/iran-independence-day-and-limits-online-politics>. For a reflective account of the Chinese situation, see: D. W. Liang, 'A new Tiananmen – but this time China's rebels are online', *The Times*, 4 Jul. 2009, <entertainment.timesonline.co.uk/tol/arts_and_entertainment/books/article6625767.ece>.

30   J. Jarvis, 'Campaign by the net, govern by the net', *The Guardian*, 22 Jan. 2009, <www.guardian.co.uk/commentisfree/2009/jan/22/obama-white-house-barackobama>.

31   L. Lessig, 'OneWebDay', *Lessig 2.0*, 23 Sep. 2008, <lessig.org/blog/2008/09/onewebday.html>.

32   Palfrey and Gasser, *Born Digital*, pp. 256–7. Although the authors concede that evidence of digital youth activism is still limited, they claim to be hopeful; see ibid., pp. 258–71 for further discussion. Cf. also the essays in W. L. Bennett (ed.), *Civic Life Online: Learning How Digital Media Can Engage Youth*, MIT Press, Cambridge, MA, 2008, <www.mitpressjournals.org/toc/dmal/-/1>.

33   Cited in J. Kiss, 'Channel 4 and Bebo launch Battlefront website in bid to inspire young people', *The Guardian*, 1 Sep. 2008, <www.guardian.co.uk/media/2008/sep/01/channel4.bebo>.

34   OECD, 'The future of the internet?', FutureInternet Channel, *YouTube*, <www.youtube.com/futureinternet>.

35   'The Linden Prize', *Linden Lab*, n. d., <lindenlab.com/lindenprize>. The joint winners, announced on 30 April, were Studio Wikitecture (which supports collaborative architectural design by geographically distributed teams) and Virtual Ability (which assists the disabled in using Second Life); see: 'Linden Lab announces co-winners of inaugural Linden Prize', *Linden Lab*, 30 Apr. 2009, <lindenlab.com/pressroom/releases/30_04_09>.

36   C. Anderson, 'Free! Why $0.00 is the future of business', *Wired*, 25 Feb. 2008, <www.wired.com/techbiz/it/magazine/16-03/ff_free?>.

37   A. Moses, 'Jail the "greedy" scam victims, says Nigerian diplomat', *The Sydney Morning Herald*, 22 Aug. 2008, <www.smh.com.au/news/web/jail-the-greedy-scam-victims-says-nigeria/2008/08/21/1219262473059.html>.

38   See for example, E. Mayo and A. Nairn, *Consumer Kids: How Big Business is Grooming Our Children for Profit*, Constable, London, 2009; K. C. Montgomery, *Generation Digital: Politics, Commerce, and Childhood in the Age of the Internet*, MIT Press, Cambridge, MA, 2007, esp. pp. 216–21; H. Skaar, 'Literacy on a social networking site', in Drotner, Siggaard Jensen and Schrøder (eds), *Informal Learning and Digital Media*, pp. 180–202.

39   Jenkins, *Convergence Culture*, p. 242; P. Ludlow and M. Wallace, *The Second Life Herald: The Virtual Tabloid that Witnessed the Dawn of the Metaverse*, MIT Press, Cambridge, MA, 2007.

40   N. Carr, 'Sharecropping the long tail', *Rough Type*, 19 Dec. 2006, <www.roughtype.com/archives/2006/12/sharecropping_t.php>; S. Mørk Petersen, 'Loser generated content: From participation to exploitation', *First Monday*, vol. 13, no. 3, 3 Mar. 2008, <firstmonday.org/htbin/cgiwrap/bin/ojs/index.php/fm/article/view/2141/1948>.

41   Palfrey and Gasser, *Born Digital*, p. 225.

42   ibid., p. 226.

43   Leadbeater, *We-Think*, pp. xi, 6.

44   J. H. Clippinger, *A Crowd of One: The Future of Individual Identity*, Public Affairs, New York, 2007, p. 183. Jeff Howe makes almost exactly the same point: 'the firm isn't so much becoming obsolete as it is evolving into just one of many deeply interconnected species in an increasingly complex ecology'; see: Howe, *Crowdsourcing*, pp. 111–12.

45   Shirky, *Here Comes Everybody*, pp. 47–8.

46   Benkler, *The Wealth of Networks*, p. 463.

47   Loewenstein, *The Blogging Revolution*, p. 159.

48   'Marching off to cyberwar', *The Economist*, 4 Dec. 2008, <www.economist.com/science/tq/displaystory.cfm?story_id=12673385>. See also: Carr, *The Big Switch*, p. 176.

49   I. Black, 'Hackers force Al-Arabiya site name change', *The Guardian*, 13 Oct. 2008, <www.guardian.co.uk/world/2008/oct/13/middleeast-internet>; A. Harper, 'Israel-Palestine conflict spills into cyberspace', *The Guardian*, 15 Jan. 2009, <www.guardian.co.uk/technology/2009/jan/15/israel-palestine-online-conflict>.

50   Friedman, *The World is Flat*, p. 8.

51   Stalder, 'Bourgeois anarchism and authoritarian democracies'. See also: The Eminent Jurists Panel on Terrorism, Counter-terrorism and Human Rights, *Assessing Damage, Urging Action*, International Commission of Jurists, Geneva, 2009, <www.icj.org/IMG/EJP-report.pdf>; A. Hirsch, 'DPP attacks approach to fighting terror', *The Guardian*, 21 Oct. 2008, <www.guardian.co.uk/politics/2008/oct/21/terrorism-uk-security>; M. Weaver, 'Former MI5 chief: Government exploits terror fears to restrict civil liberties', *The Guardian*, 17 Feb. 2009, <www.guardian.co.uk/uk/2009/feb/17/government-exploiting-terrorism-fear>.

52   Abelson, Ledeen and Lewis, *Blown to Bits*, pp. 51–5; Lessig, *Code Version 2.0*, p. 61; Stalder, 'Bourgeois anarchism and authoritarian democracies'.

53   Fons Tuinstra cited in Loewenstein, *The Blogging Revolution*, p. 205.

54   'CPJ's 2008 prison census: Online and in jail', *Committee to Protect Journalists*, 4 Dec. 2008, <cpj.org/imprisoned/cpjs-2008-census-online-journalists-now-jailed-mor.php>.

55   Abelson, Ledeen and Lewis (with reference to Robert Fano), *Blown to Bits*, p. 71.

56   M. Ahmed, 'Facebook, Bebo and MySpace "to be monitored by security services"', *The Times*, 25 Mar. 2009, <technology.timesonline.co.uk/tol/news/tech_and_web/article5973731.ece>; B. Johnson, 'What does the government know about my internet use?', *The Guardian*, 6 Apr. 2009, <www.guardian.co.uk/technology/blog/2009/apr/06/privacy-and-the-net-data-protection>; R. Ford, 'UK scraps plans for Big Brother database', *The Times*, 28 Apr. 2009, <technology.timesonline.co.uk/tol/news/tech_and_web/article6185098.ece>. Under current arrangements, the actual content of phone calls, emails or web activity is not stored.

57   President Lee Myung-Bak cited in M. Fitzpatrick, 'South Korea wants to gag the noisy internet rabble', *The Guardian*, 8 Oct. 2008, <www.guardian.co.uk/technology/2008/oct/09/news.internet>. See also: H.-S. Jung and J.-U. Limb, 'Choi suicide sparks debate about internet slander law', *JoongAng Daily*, 4 Oct. 2008, <joongangdaily.joins.com/article/view.asp?aid=2895683>; T.-H. Kim, 'Google refuses to bow to gov't pressure', *The Korea Times*, 9 Apr. 2009, <www.koreatimes.co.kr/www/news/tech/2009/04/133_42874.html>; T.-H. Kim, 'Internet users flock to foreign sites to avoid censorship', *The Korea Times*, 12 Apr. 2009, <www.koreatimes.co.kr/www/news/tech/2009/04/129_43004.html>.

58   Amnesty International, *Undermining Freedom of Expression in China: The Role of Yahoo!, Microsoft and Google*, London, Jul. 2006, <www.amnesty.org/en/library/asset/POL30/026/2006/en/dom-POL300262006en.pdf>; E. MacAskill, 'Yahoo forced to apologise to Chinese dissidents over crackdown on journalists', *The Guardian*, 14 Nov. 2007, <www.guardian.co.uk/technology/2007/nov/14/news.yahoo>; 'IPFA 2005 – Shi Tao', *Committee to Protect Journalists*, <cpj.org/awards/2005/shi-tao.php>.

59   Jerry Yang cited in P. S. Goodman, 'Yahoo says it gave China internet data', *The Washington Post*, 11 Sep. 2005, p. A30, <www.washingtonpost.com/wp-dyn/content/article/2005/09/10/AR2005091001222.html>.

60   I. MacKinnon, '£9m firewall to protect Thai king from online detractors', *The Guardian*, 30 Oct. 2008, <www.guardian.co.uk/world/2008/oct/30/firewall-king-thailand>; K. Tortermvasana, 'New ICT minister vows to curb rogue websites', *Bangkok Post*, 29 Dec. 2008, <www.bangkokpost.com/business/economics/8895/new-ict-minister-vows-to-curb-rogue-websites>; 'Thai website to protect the king', *BBC News*, 5 Feb. 2009, <news.bbc.co.uk/2/hi/asia-pacific/7871748.stm>.

61   'Global internet filtering map', *OpenNet Initiative*, <map.opennet.net/filtering-pol.html>.

62   'List of websites blocked in the People's Republic of China', *Wikipedia*, <en.wikipedia.org/wiki/List_of_websites_blocked_in_ the_People%27s_Republic_of_China> (accessed 4 Jun. 2009).

63   Xiao Qiang cited in J. Fallows, 'The connection has been reset', *The Atlantic*, Mar. 2008, <www.theatlantic.com/doc/200803/chinese-firewall>.

64   S. Ramachander, 'Internet filtering in Europe', in Deibert et al. (eds), *Access Denied*, pp. 188–9.

65   R. MacKinnon, 'China's latest internet crackdown', *RConversation*, 6 Jan. 2009, <rconversation.blogs.com/rconversation/2009/01/chinas-latest-i.html>; R. MacKinnon, 'Green Dam is breached…Now what?', *RConversation*, 2 Jul. 2009, <rconversation.blogs.com/rconversation/2009/07/green-dam-is-breachednow-what.html>.

66   Australian Communications and Media Authority, *Developments in Internet Filtering Technologies and Other Measures for Promoting Online Safety: Second Annual Report to the Minister for Broadband, Communications and the Digital Economy*, Canberra, Apr. 2009, <www.acma.gov.au/webwr/_assets/main/lib310554/developments_in_internet_filters_2ndreport.pdf>; T. Edwards and G. Griffith, 'Internet censorship and mandatory filtering', *E-Brief*, no. 5/08, Nov. 2008, New South Wales Parliamentary Library Research Service [Australia], <www.parliament.nsw.gov.au/prod/parlment/publications.nsf/0/7F8B9A55E2FC8932CA2575030083844A/$File/E%20Brief%20Internet%20Censorship.pdf>; A. Moses, 'Filtering out the fury: How government tried to gag web censor critics', *The Sydney Morning Herald*, 24 Oct. 2008, <www.smh.com.au/articles/2008/10/23/1224351430987.html>.

67   Despite massive protests, on 18 June 2009 Germany passed legislation requiring ISP filtering of the web, though the legislation currently only allows for the blocking of child pornography; see: J. York, 'Germany passes legislation to block child pornography', *OpenNet Initiative*, 22 Jun. 2009, <opennet.net/blog/2009/06/germany-passes-legislation-block-child-pornography>.

68   D. E. Bambauer, 'Filtering in Oz: Australia's foray into internet censorship', *Brooklyn Law School Legal Studies Research Papers: Working Paper Series*, Research Paper no. 125, Dec. 2008, p. 2, <papers.ssrn.com/sol3/papers.cfm?abstract_id=1319466#>.

69   Senator Stephen Conroy, whose full title is Minister for Broadband, Communications and the Digital Economy, cited in F. Foo, 'Conroy coy on filtered web content', *The Australian*, 12 Nov. 2008, <www.australianit.news.com.au/story/0,25197,24641171-15306,00.html>. See also: A. Moses, 'Labor plan to censor internet in shreds', *The Sydney Morning Herald*, 9 Dec. 2008, <www.smh.com.au/news/home/technology/labor-plan-to-censor-internet-in-shreds/2008/12/09/1228584820006.html>.

70   On adult pornography, see: A. Moses, 'Net filters may block porn and gambling sites', *The Sydney Morning Herald*, 27 Oct. 2008, <www.smh.com.au/news/technology/biztech/net-filters-may-block-porn-and-fetish-sites/2008/10/27/1224955916155.html>. On gambling, see: W. Carlisle, 'Conroy's clean feed', *Background Briefing*, ABC Radio National [Aus.], 15 Mar. 2009, <www.abc.net.au/rn/backgroundbriefing/stories/2009/2512171.htm>; Moses, 'Net filters may block porn and gambling sites'. On anorexia, see: Carlisle, 'Conroy's clean feed'; E. Harvey, 'Call to ban anorexia websites', *The Sydney Morning Herald: Life & Style*, 17 Apr. 2008, <www.smh.com.au/news/national/call-to-ban-anorexia-websites/2008/04/16/1208025283081.html>; C. Jacobs, 'Conroy comes out swinging', *PollieGraph*, 2 Apr. 2009, <newmatilda.com/polliegraph/?p=545>. On euthanasia, see: Carlisle, 'Conroy's clean feed'. The current ACMA (Australian Communications and Media Authority) blacklist, on which the expanded list is to be based, was revealed in early 2009 to contain less than 32 per cent underage images; see 'Australian government admits less than 32% of secret censorship list is related to underage images', *Wikileaks*, 26 May 2009, <wikileaks.org/wiki/Australian_government_admits_less_than_32%25_of_secret_censorship_list_is_related_to_underage_images>; also available on the *CyberLaw Blog* at: <cyberlaw.org.uk/2009/05/28/australian-government-admits-less-than-32-of-secret-censorship-list-is-related-to-underage-images/>.

71   Bambauer, 'Filtering in Oz', p. 8; P. Coroneos, 'Internet content policy and regulation in Australia', in B. Fitzgerald, F. Gao, D. O'Brien and S. X. Shi (eds), *Copyright Law, Digital Content and the Internet in the Asia-Pacific*, Sydney University Press, Sydney, 2008, p. 51,

    <eprints.qut.edu.au/archive/00013632/01/13632.pdf>.

72   Bambauer, 'Filtering in Oz', pp. 11, 17.

73   H. Lewis, 'Australian internet filtering', *Blown to Bits* [blog], 17 Oct. 2008, <www.bitsbook.com/2008/10/australian-internet-filtering/>.

74   L. Parker, 'Fears over Australia's £55m plan to censor the internet', *The Guardian*, 20 Nov. 2008, <www.guardian.co.uk/technology/2008/nov/20/australia-internet-filter-censorship>.

75   'Australian government secret ACMA internet censorship blacklist, 6 Aug. 2008', *Wikileaks*, 18 Mar. 2009, <wikileaks.org/wiki/Australian_government_secret_ACMA_internet_censorship_blacklist%2C_6_Aug_2008>. See also: 'Western internet censorship: The beginning of the end or the end of the beginning?', *Wikileaks*, 29 Mar. 2009, <wikileaks.org/wiki/Western_internet_censorship:_The_beginning_of_the_end_or_the_end_of_the_beginning%3F>.

76   Australian Liberal Party Senator Nick Minchin, Shadow Minister for Broadband, Communications and the Digital Economy, 'Labor's arbitrary internet filter plan misguided and deeply unpopular', *Liberal Party of Australia*, 25 Nov. 2008, <www.liberal.org.au/news.php?Id=2155>.

77   Australian Greens Senator Scott Ludlum cited in Moses, 'Filtering out the fury'.

78   Jack the Insider, 'Book burning in the digital age', *The Australian*, 17 Nov. 2008, <blogs.theaustralian.news.com.au/jacktheinsider/index.php/theaustralian/comments/book_burning_in_the_digital_age/>.

79   G. Philipson, 'All aboard the freedom ride', *The Sydney Morning Herald*, 2 Dec. 2008, <www.smh.com.au/news/technology/opinion/perspectives/all-aboard-the-freedom-ride/2008/12/01/1227979933431.html>.

80   G. Mulcaster, 'Opposition rises to internet filter', *The Age*, 11 Nov. 2008, <www.theage.com.au/national/opposition-rises-to-internet-filter-20081110-5lq5.html>; J. Stewart, 'Internet industry remains opposed to online filter', *Lateline*, ABC TV [Aus.], 24 Feb. 2009, <www.abc.net.au/lateline/content/2008/s2500416.htm>. See also: R. Kipps, *Submission to Prime Minister*, 2 Nov. 2008, <www.exiledmind.net/files/081102rudd.pdf>; M. Newton, 'Won't somebody think of the adults?', *Policy*, Summer 2008–2009, <www.cis.org.au/Policy/Summer08-09/newton_summer08.html>.

81   79 per cent: 'Federal government's mandatory internet filtering proposal: Netspace customer survey results', *Netspace*, 2009, <www.netspace.net.au/filtering/results.php>; 80 per cent: 'EFA's Dale Clapperton on Sunrise', *Electronic Frontiers Australia*, 29 Oct. 2008, <www.efa.org.au/2008/10/29/efas-dale-clapperton-on-sunrise/>; 86 per cent: L. Edmistone, R. Viellaris and J. Dudley-Nicholson, 'Internet filter to cause world wide wait for Aussies', *The Courier-Mail*, 29 Oct. 2008, <www.news.com.au/couriermail/story/0,23739,24567413-952,00.html>.

82   A. Moses, 'Children's welfare groups slam net filters', *The Sydney Morning Herald*, 1 Dec. 2008, <www.smh.com.au/news/home/technology/internet-censor-plan-blasted/2008/11/28/1227491813497.html>. In July 2009, Save the Children joined the National Children's & Youth Law Centre, the Australian Library and Information Association, and civil liberties groups in signing a public statement against the proposed censorship plans; see 'Active anti-censorship campaign starts', *Civil Liberties Australia*, 9 Jul. 2009, <www.cla.asn.au/0805/index.php/articles/2009/active-anti-censorship-campaign-starts>; F. Foo, 'Net filtering a $33m waste: child groups', *The Australian*, 9 Jul. 2009, <www.australianit.news.com.au/story/0,27574,25756003-15306,00.html>.

83   See Senator Conroy's comments on *Q & A*, ABC TV [Aus.], 26 Mar. 2009, <www.abc.net.au/tv/qanda/txt/s2521164.htm> and 'Blocking the net', *Insight*, SBS TV [Aus.], 31 Mar. 2009, <news.sbs.com.au/insight/episode/index/id/59>.

84   Abelson, Ledeen and Lewis, *Blown to Bits*, pp. 152–6; D. Vitaliev, 'Corporate complicity with the Great Firewall', *The Guardian*, 13 Aug. 2008, <www.guardian.co.uk/commentisfree/2008/aug/13/china.censorship>; Goldsmith and Wu, *Who Controls the Internet?*, pp. 92–6; Loewenstein, *The Blogging Revolution*, pp. 187–98.

85 J. Avila, C. Francescani and M. Harris, 'The home video Prince doesn't want you to see', *ABC News* [US], 26 Oct. 2007, <abcnews.go.com/TheLaw/Story?id=3777651>; B. Egelko, 'Woman can sue over YouTube clip de-posting', *San Francisco Chronicle*, 21 Aug. 2008, <www.sfgate.com/cgi-bin/article.cgi?f=/c/a/2008/08/20/MNU412FKRL.DTL>. For a slightly different version of this story, see: L. Lessig, *Remix: Making Art and Commerce Thrive in the Hybrid Economy*, Bloomsbury, London, 2008, pp. 1–5, <www.bloomsburyacademic.com/remix.htm>.

86 Doctorow, *Content*, esp. p. 11.

87 Benkler, *The Wealth of Networks*, esp. pp. 379–82; J. Boyle, *The Public Domain: Enclosing the Commons of the Mind*, Yale University Press, New Haven, CT, 2008, <www.thepublicdomain.org/download/>; L. Lessig, *Free Culture: How Big Media Uses Technology and the Law to Lock Down Culture and Control Creativity*, Penguin, New York, 2004.

88 Benkler, *The Wealth of Networks*, pp. 423–7; Bruns, *Blogs, Wikipedia, Second Life, and Beyond*, pp. 245–6; Doctorow, *Content*, pp. 134–5. See also: B. Andersen and M. Frenz, 'The impact of music downloads and p2p file-sharing on the purchase of music: A study for Industry Canada', *Industry Canada*, 2007, <www.ic.gc.ca/eic/site/ippd-dppi.nsf/eng/h_ip01456.html>.

89 L. Lessig, 'Prosecuting online file sharing turns a generation criminal', *US News*, 22 Dec. 2008, <www.usnews.com/articles/opinion/2008/12/22/prosecuting-online-file-sharing-turns-a-generation-criminal.html>. See also: Lessig, *Remix*, pp. xvii–xxii, 283–7, 293–4.

90 Benkler, *The Wealth of Networks*, p. 426.

91 Trent Reznor cited in F. Rose, 'Trent Reznor on *Year Zero*, planting clues, and what's ludicrous about being a musician today', *Wired*, 20 Dec. 2007, <www.wired.com/entertainment/music/magazine/16-01/ff_arg_reznor>; Trent Reznor cited in F. Rose, 'Nine Inch Nails iPhone app extends Reznor's innovative run', *Wired*, 6 Apr. 2009, <blog.wired.com/underwire/2009/04/trent-reznor-wa.html>.

92 Jarvis, *What Would Google Do?*, p. 109.

93 Moby cited in J. Selvin and N. Chonin, 'Artists blast record companies over lawsuits against downloaders', *San Francisco Chronicle*, 11 Sep. 2003, <www.sfgate.com/cgi-bin/article.cgi?f=/c/a/2003/09/11/MN12066.DTL>.

94 Bruns, *Blogs, Wikipedia, Second Life, and Beyond*, p. 275.

95 Lessig, *Code Version 2.0*, p. 4.

96 Zittrain, *The Future of the Internet*, p. 107. See also: Abelson, Ledeen and Lewis, *Blown to Bits*, pp. 210–13; T. Gillespie, *Wired Shut: Copyright and the Shape of Digital Culture*, MIT Press, Cambridge, MA, 2007.

97 Zittrain, *The Future of the Internet*, p. 27.

98 Palfrey and Gasser, *Born Digital*, p. 270.

99 Cited in Loewenstein, *The Blogging Revolution*, pp. 39, 199.

100 Associated Press, 'Yahoo criticized in case of jailed dissident', *The New York Times*, 7 Nov. 2007, <www.nytimes.com/2007/11/07/technology/07yahoo.html>.

101 Loewenstein, *The Blogging Revolution*, p. 195.

102 N. Scola, 'Return of the Global Online Freedom Act (and some strange politics with it)', *techPresident*, 8 May 2009, <techpresident.com/blog-entry/return-global-online-freedom-act-and-some-strange-politics-it>; H. Jones, 'EU media chief rules out internet freedom law', *Reuters*, 3 Feb. 2009, <www.reuters.com/article/technologyNews/idUSTRE5124SB20090203>.

103 T. Reynolds and S. Wunsch-Vincent, *Broadband Growth and Policies in OECD Countries*, OECD, 2008, p. 13, <www.scribd.com/doc/3040556/OECD-report-on-Broadband-Growth-and-Policies-Full-Report>.

104 Abelson, Ledeen and Lewis, *Blown to Bits*, pp. 161–5.

105 On Wikipedia, see: D. Smith and J. Revill, 'Wikipedia defies China's censors', *The Guardian*, 10 Sep. 2006, <www.guardian.co.uk/technology/2006/sep/10/news.china>; R. MacKinnon, 'Jimbo Wales: Google's China mistake', *RConversation*, 4 Aug. 2007, <rconversation.blogs.com/rconversation/2007/08/jimmy-wales-goo.html>. On WordPress,

see: Loewenstein, *The Blogging Revolution*, p. 191. On Google, see: Associated Press, 'Tech companies embrace human rights guidelines', *The Sydney Morning Herald*, 28 Oct. 2008, <www.smh.com.au/news/technology/biztech/tech-companies-embrace-human-rights-guidelines/2008/10/28/1224956028359.html>.

106   Abelson, Ledeen and Lewis, *Blown to Bits*, p. 254.

107   Kim, 'Google refuses to bow to gov't pressure'.

108   'Frequently Asked Questions', *Global Network Initiative*, 2008, <www.globalnetworkinitiative.org/faq/index.php>.

109   Y. Benkler, 'The university in the networked economy and society: Challenges and opportunities', in R. N. Katz (ed.), *The Tower and the Cloud: Higher Education in the Age of Cloud Computing*, EDUCAUSE, 2008, p. 55, <net.educause.edu/ir/library/pdf/PUB7202f.pdf>.

110   Gillmor, *We the Media*, p. 219.

6 – Many *baas* & ^^^^^: An ecological lens

1   Stald, 'Mobile identity', p. 151; J. Stark, 'Tired teens risking their hearts', *The Sydney Morning Herald*, 19 Aug. 2008, <www.smh.com.au/news/athome/tired-teens-risking-their-hearts/2008/08/18/1218911686857.html>.

2   Palfrey and Gasser, *Born Digital*, p. 187.

3   On China, see: J. Macartney, 'Internet addiction made an official disorder in China', *The Times*, 11 Nov. 2008, <www.timesonline.co.uk/tol/news/world/asia/article5125324.ece>; J. Jiang, 'Inside China's fight against internet addiction', *Time*, 28 Jan. 2009, <www.time.com/time/world/article/0,8599,1874380,00.html>. On South Korea, see: J. J. Block, 'Issues for DSM-V: Internet addiction', *The American Journal of Psychiatry*, vol. 165, no. 3, Mar. 2008, pp. 306–7; M. Fackler, 'In Korea, a boot camp cure for web obsession', *The New York Times*, 18 Nov. 2007, <www.nytimes.com/2007/11/18/technology/18rehab.html>.

4   M. Griffiths, 'Internet addiction – Time to be taken seriously?', *Addiction Research*, vol. 8, no. 5, Oct. 2000, pp. 413–18; J. Morahan-Martin, 'Internet use and abuse and psychological problems', in Joinson et al. (eds), *The Oxford Handbook of Internet Psychology*, pp. 331–45.

5   J. Markoff, 'What's really up, Doc?', *The Sydney Morning Herald*, 8 Dec. 2008, <www.smh.com.au/news/technology/web/whats-really-up-doc/2008/12/06/1228257375359.html>; Small and Vorgan, *iBrain*, pp. 173–5.

6   On blogging, see: J. Moorhead, 'Online lifelines', *The Guardian*, 9 Sep. 2008, <www.guardian.co.uk/lifeandstyle/2008/sep/09/healthandwellbeing.health>. On social networking, see: C. Cain Miller, 'Social networking for patients', *The New York Times*, 24 Oct. 2008, <bits.blogs.nytimes.com/2008/10/24/social-networking-for-patients/>. On transplants, see: H. Kaur Grewal, 'Facebook is new tool in transplant donor appeals', *The Guardian*, 15 Dec. 2008, <www.guardian.co.uk/technology/2008/dec/15/facebook-transplant-donor-campaign>.

7   R. Champeau, 'UCLA study finds that searching the internet increases brain function', *UCLA Newsroom*, 14 Oct. 2008, <newsroom.ucla.edu/portal/ucla/ucla-study-finds-that-searching-64348.aspx>.

8   S. Greenfield, *ID: The Quest for Identity in the 21ˢᵗ Century*, Sceptre, London, 2008, esp. pp. 26–31; Small and Vorgan, *iBrain*, esp. pp. 1–9.

9   N. K. Hayles, 'Hyper and deep attention: The generational divide in cognitive modes', *Profession*, 2007, pp. 187–99; Small and Vorgan, *iBrain*, pp. 20–2; Tapscott, *Grown Up Digital*, pp. 29–30, 97–106. Despite the drawbacks of multitasking, as discussed in Chapter 4, some authors suggest it may be possible to adapt to it; see: N. S. Baron, 'Adjusting the volume: Technology and multitasking in discourse control', in Katz (ed.), *Handbook of Mobile Communication Studies*, p. 184 (cf. Baron, *Always On*, pp. 39–40); Small and Vorgan, *iBrain*, pp. 21–2, 32–4, 137. On creativity, see: Small and Vorgan, *iBrain*, pp. 69–71.

10   On ADD/ADHD, see: Small and Vorgan, *iBrain*, pp. 64–8; cf. also Hayles, 'Hyper and deep attention'. On autistic tendencies, see: Small and Vorgan, *iBrain*, pp. 2 , 71–4.

11   Gary Small cited in J. Kiss, 'The internet is changing our brains', *The Guardian*, 27 Oct. 2008, <www.guardian.co.uk/media/pda/2008/oct/27/socialnetworking>.

12   Greenfield, *ID*, pp. 12–13.

13   Carr, *The Big Switch*, pp. 216–17; Small and Vorgan, *iBrain*, p. 187.

14   Larry Page and Sergey Brin cited in Carr, *The Big Switch*, p. 213.

15   N. Alderman, 'Death to death', *The Guardian*, 28 Oct. 2008, <www.guardian.co.uk/technology/2008/oct/28/naomi-alderman-living-forever>. See also: Doctorow, *Content*, pp. 145–58.

16   See for example, N. K. Hayles, *How We Became Posthuman: Virtual Bodies in Cybernetics, Literature, and Informatics*, University of Chicago Press, Chicago, 1999.

17   Carr, *The Big Switch*, p. 215.

18   The Parliamentary Office of Science and Technology [UK], 'ICT and CO_2 emissions', *Postnote*, no. 319, Dec. 2008, <www.parliament.uk/documents/upload/postpn319.pdf>.

19   B. Johnson, 'Web providers must limit internet's carbon footprint, say experts', *The Guardian*, 3 May 2009, <www.guardian.co.uk/technology/2009/may/03/internet-carbon-footprint>.

20   J. Leake and R. Woods, 'Revealed: The environmental impact of Google searches', *The Times*, 11 Jan. 2009, <technology.timesonline.co.uk/tol/news/tech_and_web/article5489134.ece>.

21   McAfee/ICF, *The Carbon Footprint of Email Spam Report*, McAfee, Santa Clara, CA, 2009, <img.en25.com/Web/McAfee/CarbonFootprint_28pg_web_REV.PDF>.

22   N. Carr, 'Avatars consume as much electricity as Brazilians', *Rough Type*, 5 Dec. 2006, <www.roughtype.com/archives/2006/12/avatars_consume.php>.

23   A. Finn, 'Technological meltdown', *The Guardian*, 7 Oct. 2008, <www.guardian.co.uk/money/2008/oct/07/workandcareers.waste>; B. Walsh, 'E-waste not', *Time*, 8 Jan. 2009, <www.time.com/time/magazine/article/0,9171,1870485,00.html>; R. Wray, 'Breeding toxins from dead PCs', *The Guardian*, 6 May 2008, <www.guardian.co.uk/environment/2008/may/06/waste.pollution>.

24   'On its way, at last', *The Economist*, 9 Oct. 2008, <www.economist.com/business/displaystory.cfm?story_id=12376821&fsrc>.

25   M. Ahmed, 'Google search finds seafaring solution', *The Times*, 15 Sep. 2008, <technology.timesonline.co.uk/tol/news/tech_and_web/article4753389.ece>; J. Cheng, 'Google envisions future of floating, blue-green data centers', *Ars Technica*, 1 May 2009, <arstechnica.com/hardware/news/2009/05/floating-data-center-patent-granted-to-google.ars>.

26   F. Foo, 'Energy rating plan to cut tech carbon emissions', *The Australian*, 14 Oct. 2008, <www.australianit.news.com.au/story/0,25197,24490955-15306,00.html>.

27   M. Wertheim, *The Pearly Gates of Cyberspace: A History of Space from Dante to the Internet*, Virago, London, 1999, p. 254.

28   M. Benedikt, 'Introduction', in M. Benedikt (ed.), *Cyberspace: First Steps*, MIT Press, Cambridge, MA, 1991, pp. 14–18; N. Stenger, 'Mind is a leaking rainbow', in Benedikt (ed.), *Cyberspace*, p. 52.

29   S. E. George, *Religion and Technology in the 21ˢᵗ Century: Faith in the E-World*, Information Science Publishing, Hershey, PA, 2006, esp. pp. x, 82–90; D. M. Levy, *Scrolling Forward: Making Sense of Documents in the Digital Age*, Arcade, New York, 2001, pp. 199–200; Wertheim, *The Pearly Gates of Cyberspace*, esp. pp. 251–80.

30   Carr, *The Big Switch*, p. 108.

31   Joshua Quittner cited in Turner, *From Counterculture to Cyberculture*, pp. 218–19.

32   B. E. Brasher (with reference to Jennifer Cobb), *Give Me that Online Religion*, Jossey-Bass, San Francisco, 2001, p. 40.

33   J. Hammerman, *thelordismyshepherd.com: Seeking God in Cyberspace*, Simcha Press, Deerfield Beach, FL, pp. 85, 116.

34   'Internet can warn of ecological changes', *Stockholm University*, 19 Mar. 2009, <www.su.se/english/about/press/press_releases/internet_can_warn_of_ecological_changes>.

35   Elon Musk cited in K. Mayo and P. Newcomb, 'How the web was won', *Vanity Fair*, Jul. 2008, <www.vanityfair.com/culture/features/2008/07/internet200807>.

36   'A doctor in your pocket', *The Economist*, 16 Apr. 2009, <www.economist.com/specialreports/displaystory.cfm?story_id= 13437958>.

37   Levy, *Scrolling Forward*, p. 186.

SELECT BIBLIOGRAPHY

I: Books

Abelson, H., Ledeen, K. and Lewis, H., *Blown to Bits: Your Life, Liberty, and Happiness After the Digital Explosion*, Addison-Wesley, Upper Saddle River, NJ, 2008.

Baron, N. S., *Always On: Language in an Online and Mobile World*, Oxford University Press, New York, 2008.

Benkler, Y., *The Wealth of Networks: How Social Production Transforms Markets and Freedom*, Yale University Press, New Haven, CT, 2006.

Bruns, A., *Blogs, Wikipedia, Second Life, and Beyond: From Production to Produsage*, Peter Lang, New York, 2008.

Buckingham, D., (ed.), *Youth, Identity, and Digital Media*, MIT Press, Cambridge, MA, 2008. Open Access edition: <www.mitpressjournals.org/toc/dmal/-/6>.

Carr, N., *The Big Switch: Rewiring the World, From Edison to Google*, W. W. Norton, New York, 2008.

Crystal, D., *Txtng: The Gr8 Db8*, Oxford University Press, Oxford, 2008.

Deibert, R., Palfrey, J., Rohozinski, R. and Zittrain, J., *Access Denied: The Practice and Policy of Global Internet Filtering*, MIT Press, Cambridge, MA, 2008. Open Access edition: <opennet.net/accessdenied>.

Doctorow, C., *Content: Selected Essays on Technology, Creativity, Copyright, and the Future of the Future*, Tachyon, San Francisco, 2008.

Friedman, T. L., *The World is Flat: A Brief History of the Twenty-first Century*, New edn., Picador, New York, 2007.

Howe, J., *Crowdsourcing: Why the Power of the Crowd is Driving the Future of Business*, Crown Business, New York, 2008.

Jarvis, J., *What Would Google Do?*, Collins Business, New York, 2009.

Jenkins, H., *Convergence Culture: Where Old and New Media Collide*, New edn., New York University Press, New York, 2008.

Lankshear, C. and Knobel, M., *New Literacies: Everyday Practices and Classroom Learning*, 2nd edn., Open University Press, Maidenhead, Berkshire, 2006.

Leadbeater, C. (and 257 other people), *We-Think*, Profile Books, London, 2008.

Lessig, L., *Code Version 2.0*, Basic Books, New York, 2006. Open Access edition: <codev2.cc/download+remix/>.

——, *Remix: Making Art and Commerce Thrive in the Hybrid Economy*, Bloomsbury, London, 2008. Open Access edition: <www.bloomsburyacademic.com/remix.htm>.

Lih, A., *The Wikipedia Revolution: How a Bunch of Nobodies Created the World's Greatest Encyclopedia*, Aurum, London, 2009.

Ling, R., *New Tech, New Ties: How Mobile Communication is Reshaping Social Cohesion*, MIT Press, Cambridge, MA, 2008.

Loewenstein, A., *The Blogging Revolution*, Melbourne University Press, Melbourne, 2008.

Palfrey, J. and Gasser, U., *Born Digital: Understanding the First Generation of Digital Natives*, Basic Books, New York, 2008.

Shirky, C., *Here Comes Everybody: The Power of Organizing Without Organizations*, Allen Lane, New York, 2008.

Warschauer, M., *Laptops and Literacy: Learning in the Wireless Classroom*, Teachers College Press, New York, 2006.

Weinberger, D., *Everything is Miscellaneous: The Power of the New Digital Disorder*, Times Books, New York, 2007.

Zittrain, J., *The Future of the Internet and How to Stop It*, Allen Lane, London, 2008. Open Access edition: <futureoftheinternet.org/download>.

II: Blogs

boyd, d. (main focus: social networking), *Apophenia*, <www.zephoria.org/thoughts/>.

Carr, N. ('The Big Switch'), *Rough Type*, <www.roughtype.com>.

Doctorow, C. ('Content'), *Craphound*, <craphound.com>.

Dudeney, G. (main focus: Second Life and language teaching), *That'SLife*, <slife.dudeney.com>.

Fake, C. (co-founder of Flickr), *Caterina.net*, <www.caterina.net>.

Howe, J. ('Crowdsourcing'), *Crowdsourcing*, <crowdsourcing.typepad.com>.

Jarvis, J. ('What Would Google Do?'), *BuzzMachine*, <www.buzzmachine.com>.

Jenkins, H. ('Convergence Culture'), *Confessions of an Aca-Fan*, <www.henryjenkins.org>.

Lessig, L. ('Code Version 2.0'/'Remix'), *Lessig 2.0: Blog*, <www.lessig.org/blog/>.

Lewis, H. ('Blown to Bits'), *Blown to Bits: Blog*, <www.bitsbook.com/blog/>.

Lih, A. ('The Wikipedia Revolution'), *andrew lih*, <www.andrewlih.com/blog/>.

MacKinnon, R. (main focus: internet in China), *RConversation*, <rconversation.blogs.com>.

Newmark, C. (founder of craigslist), *cnewmark*, <www.cnewmark.com>.

O'Reilly, T. ('web 2.0'), *O'Reilly Radar: Tim O'Reilly*, <radar.oreilly.com/tim/>.

Palfrey, J. ('Born Digital'), *John Palfrey*, <blogs.law.harvard.edu/palfrey/>.

Shirky, C. ('Here Comes Everybody'), *Clay Shirky*, <www.shirky.com/weblog/>.

Wales, J. (co-founder of Wikipedia), *Jimmy Wales*, <blog.jimmywales.com>.

Weinberger, D. ('Everything is Miscellaneous'), *JOHO: The Blog!*, <www.hyperorg.com/blogger/>.

Zittrain, J. ('The Future of the Internet'), *The Future of the Internet: Blog*, <futureoftheinternet.org/blog/>.

III: News Forums

Creative Economy (main focus: new research on technology and education), <www.apo.org.au/creative-economy>.

Electronic Frontier Foundation (main focus: civil liberties online), <www.eff.org>.

Electronic Frontiers Australia (main focus: civil liberties online), <www.efa.org.au>.

Pew Internet (main focus: new research on the impact of the internet), <www.pewinternet.org>.

IV: Microblogs

Many web 2.0 innovators and commentators have Twitter feeds: danah boyd (main focus: social networking), Cory Doctorow ('Content'), Gavin Dudeney (main focus: Second Life and language teaching), Dan Gillmor ('We the Media'), Jeff Howe ('Crowdsourcing'), Jeff Jarvis ('What Would Google Do?'), Henry Jenkins ('Convergence Culture'), Charles Leadbeater ('We-Think'), Andrew Lih ('The Wikipedia Revolution'), Rebecca MacKinnon (main focus: internet in China), Craig Newmark (founder of craigslist), Pierre Omidyar (founder of eBay), Tim O'Reilly ('web 2.0'), John Palfrey ('Born Digital'), Philip Rosedale (creator of Second Life), Clay Shirky ('Here Comes Everybody'), Biz Stone (co-founder of Twitter), Linda Stone ('continuous partial attention'), Don Tapscott ('Grown Up Digital'), Jimmy Wales (co-founder of Wikipedia), David Weinberger ('Everything is Miscellaneous') and Jonathan Zittrain ('The Future of the Internet'), to name a few. You can use the Search function to locate many others.

V: Updates

For updates, you're welcome to take a look at the *E-language* wiki about digital technologies in education (<e-language.wikispaces.com>) or to follow me on Twitter (<twitter.com/OzMark17>).

INDEX

ABOUT THE AUTHOR

Mark Pegrum is an assistant professor in the Graduate School of Education at The University of Western Australia, where he teaches in the area of e-learning. His research focuses on the increasing integration of web 2.0 and mobile technologies into everyday life, and examines the pedagogical, social and sociopolitical implications of phenomena such as blogs and wikis, podcasts and video mashups, social networking sites and virtual worlds. Mark is a co-ordinator of the Third Spaces in Online Discussion project, which focuses on cross-cultural interaction in virtual classrooms. His previous book, co-edited with Joe Lockard, was entitled *Brave New Classrooms: Democratic Education and the Internet*, and was published by Peter Lang, New York, in 2007. He currently teaches in Perth, Hong Kong and Singapore and has given presentations on e-learning in Australia and New Zealand, East and Southeast Asia, and the UK and Europe. Further information on his work can be found on the *E-language* wiki at: <e-language. wikispaces.com>.